THE QUEST FOR THE ULTIMATE GRAND SLAM

THE QUEST FOR THE ULTIMATE GRAND SLAM

MIKE CATT'S YEAR

MIKE CATT
AND LEONARD STALL

MAINSTREAM
PUBLISHING
EDINBURGH AND LONDON

Cover photographs © Allsport and *The Bath Chronicle*

First published in 1995 by
MAINSTREAM PUBLISHING COMPANY (EDINBURGH) LTD
7 Albany Street
Edinburgh EH1 3UG

ISBN 1 85158 788 8

A catalogue record for this book is available from the British Library

Typeset in 12/14pt Perpetua

Printed and bound in Great Britain by Butler and Tanner Ltd, Frome

Mike dedicates this book to his brothers, for their support

Leonard dedicates it to Geneviève, his wife

Contents

ACKNOWLEDGEMENTS

Thanks to:

- Roger Marshall, for reading, re-reading and editing the manuscript, and for his moral support!
- South African Airways
- Cellnet
- Dave Rogers at Allsport
- Tracy Murray, Mandy Keegan and Annie for their transcription work
- Noel and Stuart McQuitty and Gullivers Travel for helping me in South Africa
- Fiona Foster at Karen Earl Ltd
- The English rugby press corps, and their newspapers, for filling in the holes so well when my memory played tricks
- Malcolm Pearce, Gill Wilson and Johnsons News Ltd
- John Hall and Joan Budge at Bath Rugby Football Club
- Jackie Maitland at *The Bath Chronicle*
- *and, of course, Mike's girlfriend, Debbie*

Catt the Beer Monster
BY JOHN HALL

Mike Catt is one of those annoying people who are good at everything. He also likes to party!

Catty was on tour with England in South Africa in July 1994, and afterwards he stayed on 'at home' to see family and friends. That's when we started to receive all sorts of reports back in Bath that he was drinking and partying just a bit too much for his own good. It came as no surprise, as he is well known among his team-mates as a beer monster. But the Catt consumption levels, closely monitored by my secret agents in South Africa, began to cause me some alarm. As his Bath skipper, I was concerned he would come back for the start of the new season unfit, heavier, and slower.

I thought no more about it, concentrating instead on my own pre-season build-up, and my own fitness. I had never trained so hard for a new season. I was the fittest I had ever been, and I was going to be the fittest man in the squad, or so I thought.

When I met Mike on his return from South Africa it appeared that he had not put on a single pound in weight, much to my surprise. Then came our first Bath training session of the new campaign, and Ged Roddy put us through our paces, setting us one of his gruelling training schedules that normally lasts around 20 minutes. I was really pleased with my 19-minute effort, until Mike did it in 15 minutes and beat everybody! So much for dedication. How does he do it?

Soon after, the Bath team travelled to Barbados for a mini-tour. It wasn't long before a beach salesman had signed me up for a trip around the bay on water-skis, and I persuaded Mike to join me. 'I haven't done much of that,' Catty warned. We wandered down to the boat, and he decided to go first so I threw him over the two skis. 'I only want one,' he said, and proceeded to ski all around the bay and back again on just one ski, without falling off. He can be so irritating. He was even good at Caribbean dancing!

Mike came to Bath in November 1992. I remember one of our scouts at the Rec, David Jenkins, asked me whether I'd seen the useful new player from Stroud, Mike Catt. I had watched him in training and thought that he looked quite sharp, but it wasn't until I saw him in an early First XV game that I really started to take notice. He made some devastating breaks and forced himself into the selection reckoning almost immediately.

He spent a lot of time with the squad up at Bath University, training and socialising with us all. But he was always quite quiet in those days. After early-morning training we'd have breakfast and then relax for a while and take the mickey out of each other, the Bath way. Mike was always around at the university, and it soon became obvious that he was going to be part of the Bath set-up for a long time to come and a future star.

I particularly remember Mike's Courage League début for Bath against Gloucester. Stuart Barnes was injured, and Mike came in at fly-half and had an outstanding game. The press was all over him after that, and it was definitely the launch pad for Catty's success. It's all very well to reckon a player after seeing him in training, or playing in a non-Courage League game, but he came through this high-pressure league match with flying colours.

He made further strides in the Bath pre-season tour of Canada at the beginning of the 1993–94 season. Stuart Barnes couldn't go and Mike slotted in at fly-half. He was the star of the tour, and it elevated him from being just another good player with potential, to being a player who had to be included in the side.

Of all the games Catty has played for Bath, one stands out more than any other. This was the Pilkington Cup semi-final against Harlequins at the Stoop during the 1993–94 season. It was one of the greatest games of my career, and we won at the death, 26–25. Mike showed his class, and it was him that made the difference between winning and losing. I can remember Mike leaving Will Carling for dead at one point, and it led to Jon Callard scoring.

Tony Swift and I were interviewed on *Rugby Special* after the end of this season (as two retiring old boys) and Tony was asked which was the best Bath XV he had ever played in. He picked out that 1993–94 team because of the quality in midfield. Stuart Barnes, Phil de Glanville and Mike were outstanding that season, and Mike in particular had a huge part to play in our success, especially as Jerry Guscott was injured.

Despite this high praise, Mike's best position is at full-back as far as I am concerned. He has a little more time and space at full-back, and it suits his game. Mike's a good all-round footballer, but I think his greatest attribute is his running into space from deep.

He only has one weakness, kicking with his left foot – as we found out against Italy in the World Cup – but that's something that can be worked on!

There are demanding times ahead for Mike, and probably all good young players in rugby union. Questions will have to be answered: is the game to become professional, semi-professional or remain amateur? Will players get paid, and will the money on offer be enough? Will they need a job as well?

Mike will need people he can trust around him, and in my new rôle as team manager at Bath this season, and with a new structure in place, I hope that I can help.

One way or another, I'm sure that Mike Catt will be a star that shines for a long time to come.

JOHN HALL WAS MIKE CATT'S BATH CAPTAIN UNTIL HE RETIRED AT THE END OF
LAST SEASON. HE HAS RECENTLY BEEN APPOINTED THE NEW HONORARY
BATH TEAM MANAGER

Mike Catt has played every English rugby enthusiast's fantasy this season. He has made a telling contribution to the continued success of Bath RFC, taken part in a memorable England Grand Slam, and played in what could be the first of many World Cup campaigns for his adopted country.

That's not bad for a man who has only recently turned 24.

Mike first came to England as a young holiday-maker three years ago, without a pair of rugby boots in his luggage, and the great game the furthest thing from his mind. It was meant to be a short visit, staying with relatives, travelling the UK, and widening his horizons. But he did not return to live in Port Elizabeth on the sunny South African coast, the place he still thinks of as home, preferring to stay in the beautiful city of Bath and concentrate on improving his rugby – a lifelong sporting passion.

Born and raised a South African, Mike wears the red rose thanks to his English mother, Anne, who was born in the home counties. Her nationality gave Mike the chance to claim a British passport, and eventually don the England jersey.

His rich all-round talent and enthusiasm have brought Mike fame this year. They could also bring him rich monetary rewards in the future.

He may not be the tallest international full-back at 5ft 10ins, or the heaviest at 13st 8lbs, but in only two full seasons Michael John Catt or 'Catty', as he is widely known, has climbed to the top of the rugby ladder – two rungs at a time – with the sort of speed and agility he shows on the field. It has been a remarkable success story and there is more, much more, to come.

LEONARD STALL, JULY 1995

As a player Mike Catt was one of the all-round stars of last year, and the way he is progressing will probably make him one of the biggest stars England has ever seen. I think Mike has every potential to be one of the world's greats by the time he retires.

He has a bit of everything, including a bit of the Afrikaner way which gives him an ultra-competitive edge. He's also fast, and has good hands – for all those reasons Mike Catt is going to the top.

GARETH CHILCOTT

I JUST HOPE I DON'T WAKE UP IN A MINUTE!

This 1994–95 season has been like a dream come true for me, despite it being a controversial season off the field.

Since I returned from my first full England tour of South Africa in July 1994, so much has happened, and so quickly.

Stuart Barnes retired at the end of the 1993–94 league season which meant I became the first-choice fly-half for Bath in only my second full campaign for the club.

Throughout the season there was a great deal of pressure on the Bath team. Stuart Barnes, Richard Hill and Gareth Chilcott had all retired, and there was also a new team coach at the Rec, Brian Ashton, bravely following in the footsteps of Jack Rowell – surely an impossible act to follow. It was thought that the new, young and inexperienced players, as well as the coach, would struggle to fill the size tens of these Bath legends, and it was a daunting challenge for the new squad.

Yet the Bath crowd still expected silverware at the end of the season and, having set the standard in rugby union for so long, nothing less than another league and cup double would do.

Off the field, I got caught up in my first tabloid scandal at the beginning of the season – hopefully it will be my last! The *Mail on Sunday* broke a story which claimed I had been paid for playing in South Africa. It really opened my eyes and helped me to grow up. Looking back, I was horribly naïve and trusting. After the interview with the *Mail on Sunday* freelance journalist, I never thought anything more about it until I read the papers the following weekend. My world was turned upside down in the time it took me to read the story.

Fortunately, it was all resolved, and in the final analysis I thought I was very well treated by the rugby authorities; certainly the RFU were very supportive of me. Otherwise it could have ended my Bath and England rugby career before it had even begun, and I would probably have been back on the beach in South Africa by now.

At the beginning of the season I knew that I was in the England squad, and lady luck dealt me a kind hand when I came on as a replacement for Paul Hull in the international against Canada, with only 20 minutes gone. With time to make my mark on the game, and space to run with the ball, you could say that I took my chance. But the Five Nations Championship was my real breakthrough. Being chosen for that first game of the tournament against Ireland was thrilling, and it was a big confidence booster to be chosen at full-back ahead of Paul, who had done nothing at all wrong in the games he played. Having watched the Five Nations on television at home in South Africa when I was young, playing for the England team against the Irish, French, Welsh and Scottish XVs was extraordinary, and it was a great honour to play a part in the Grand Slam decider – the Calcutta Cup game against Scotland.

Bath were disappointed to lose the Courage League title and finish runners-up to Leicester, but once again we won the game's major knock-out tournament, the Pilkington Cup. Having not performed well all season, we really pulled it out of the bag in the cup final at Twickenham.

Sadly, I didn't play in the Pilkington Cup final because I had injured a hamstring and felt that I really needed to rest it for the trip to South Africa in search of the ultimate prize, the World Cup. Retiring Bath skipper John Hall also missed out through injury in what would have been a fitting final appearance for a great club captain.

It was a cup final we felt that we had to win. If we had come home to Bath empty-handed, it would have been the first time in years that the club had won nothing. The entire performance was a terrific team effort and a credit to another retiring Bath superstar, Tony Swift, one of the club game's top finishers right up to the end of his career. It showed the critics that Bath still set the pace in English domestic rugby, and that we'll be a force to be reckoned with for many years to come.

But there was a massive dampener on the day – the sacking of Will Carling, which I felt was a fiasco. It obviously wasn't right of Will to call the members of the RFU committee '57 old farts' on the television, but the subsequent course of events was a farce. More of that later!

The season ended, of course, with the incredible experience of going to the World Cup and playing at the highest level in South Africa, my birthplace. It was easily the highlight of my rugby career so far, and a memory which will stay with me forever.

I hope you will enjoy sharing the many highs and lows of my season. Most of the book was written in the build-up to the World Cup, after the Bath season had ended. The South African experience is in diary-style, and is therefore written as events unfold. I apologise, in advance, if my memory has played tricks with the timing of events or with names. It has all happened for me so fast – in just two and a half years – that it's sometimes difficult to believe, let alone remember. It's been so good so far. I just hope I don't wake up in a minute!

MIKE CATT

ONE

Mike Catt, the Kitten

I know a lot of people don't think much of the windy city of Port Elizabeth, but I was born there on 17 September 1971, not far away from the Boet Erasmus Stadium which is one of the best-known South African Test Match grounds.

For the first four or five years of my life we lived in Humewood, which is just along the beach front in Port Elizabeth. Later, we moved closer into town.

When I was young, I lived with my mum, dad and three brothers — in descending order — Douglas the oldest, Peter, myself and Richard, the youngest.

My mother was born and raised in England's home counties, my father in South Africa. He met and married my mother in England, where my two older brothers, Douglas and Peter, were born, and then they went back to live on the eastern Cape shortly before myself, and then Richard, showed our faces to the sun for the first time.

My mum, Anne, was divorced from my dad, James (better known as Jimmy), when I was 13. We stayed with her while we were at high school. Dad has since remarried, but not my mum. She has a lodger, my 22-year-old younger brother, Richard, who still lives with her, although he is set to come to England to play scrum-half for Bath RFC later on next season, following in big brother's footsteps. Two young Catts will probably constitute a litter!

My first school was Walmer Nursery School in Port Elizabeth, which I can remember well and really enjoyed. I can recall having a big bad crush on a girl called Pauline, who I used to call

'PawPaw'. In fact, I met a lot of my friends there, people who are still my friends today, and who help me keep my feet on the ground. Most of them are still in South Africa, although some have moved up to Johannesburg where jobs are easier to find and generally a lot better paid than those in Port Elizabeth.

PE, as Port Elizabeth is known by everyone in South Africa, is a very relaxed and calm place. You could describe it as very laid back. The trouble is that the only things really going for PE are the beautiful beaches. The beach fronts and the bars on them are magic, but the only other attraction in PE is the big university, UPE.

I did all my schooling in Port Elizabeth, which I still think of as home. After nursery school in Walmer, I went to Grey Junior School at the age of six, and later on to Grey High School on the same campus.

Sport was a big thing even when we were very small, especially for the four Catt boys. We used to kick balls around, and when we didn't have a ball handy we would kick each other around!

Rugby was always the big game at home when we were growing up. At that stage black Africans were not playing rugby and it was very racist in that sense when I was young. Now, thankfully, it is beginning to change, and I believe the World Cup has helped, and will continue to help, accelerate the speed of change.

Neither were there any black Africans at Grey. It wasn't until 1990 that they were allowed into the school for the first time, and therefore when I was a boy at school we never used to play against the blacks in a sporting environment. The only occasions where we did get to play against black children were outside school, playing club football. We played for PE City from Under-10 level to Under-16s, and in this club environment teams were already fully integrated.

We started playing rugby at school from the age of six or seven, and played barefoot all the way through to Under-13s. It was very competitive even from such a young age, with fanatical parents generally the biggest competitors of all! In South Africa there are few things more important than rugby, other than to be the best and to win.

Each day, we attended junior school from 8 a.m. to 2 p.m., and from 2.30 p.m. to 5 p.m. – we would play sport whatever the weather. We practised rugby on Mondays and Wednesdays, and on Tuesdays and Thursdays we would generally go diving or play football.

At high school, we would begin classes at 8 a.m. and go through until 2.45 p.m., and then play sport from 3.30 p.m. to 5 p.m. Again, we played rugby twice a week. In the summer we played cricket, as well as being active in athletics, triathlon and diving.

Grey Junior School and Grey High School are known collectively as Grey, and it is still regarded as one of the best schools in South Africa. When I was there it was considered a very 'English' school, and there was a big rivalry between the English and the Afrikaners, even when we were young. I consider Afrikaners 'hard core' people, generally arrogant, aggressive, narrow-minded and hard. Rugby is often the most important thing in their lives, or at least it appears to be, and many of the parents will virtually beat the game into their children. It was unbelievable when I was at school. Even now, with the country in the world media spotlight, most people outside South Africa fail to comprehend just how important the game of rugby is in this nation's consciousness. It is certainly more than just a sport, more than a game; many call it a religion.

We had one rival school that we used to play against regularly, Grey Bloem in Bloemfontein, where the contests were always big, bruising derby clashes. It was really tough, yet we were only young kids.

Our parents, on the other hand, never forced sport on us, they never needed to. My love for sport and competition was passed down from my older brothers, and they taught me the rudiments of every sport or game we played. Like them, I have loved rugby for as long as I can remember.

All four of us were lucky to be natural athletes and were all fairly successful in the sports we played. But we all wanted to be the best at everything we did. And, when it came to sport, we did a great deal. My older brother, Peter, was an accomplished South African triathlete. He represented Eastern Province in triathlon, athletics and diving, as well as representing the Province at soccer at Under-16 level. I followed in his footsteps and did all of these sports for Eastern Province as well, and in all of the different age groups. I used to specialise in the 800 metres, the 3,000 metres, and the 3,000-metres steeplechase at school, as well as cross-country. We also did a lot of life-saving too. It was an outdoor life.

Peter was very competitive at everything. He used to hate it when I beat him, and as I was his younger brother it became my goal in life! The two-year age gap was big enough to give Peter the incentive he needed to win at all costs; after all, defeat by a younger brother was more than just humiliating. It was the same for my little brother, Richard, who is two years younger than me.

The Catt brothers were very close and used to play a lot of sport together, particularly as none of us were very academically minded. My mum tried hard to get us to do our school work, but it was an uphill struggle – we just wanted to play sport, all of the time.

Even when we were young we used to get up out of bed at 6 a.m. and do an hour's speed work or skills training on the athletics track before school. When we decided that we wanted to get up in the morning to train, dad would ensure we did, but he never made us do it.

I was at Grey until I was 18 years old. Unlike the education process in England, there is no option of 'getting out' at 16; we have to go through to finish matriculation at 18. After your final exams, you generally go on to college, technikon or university.

If you played rugby seriously, as I did, you could get into a school or a university without too much trouble, in fact, it was surprisingly easy. As my best subject at school was woodwork, it was just as well I was a useful sportsman, although I did learn to speak a little Afrikaans during my schooldays, which came in useful when I needed a few choice words on England's tour of South Africa in 1994.

Indeed, if you are a top sportsman in South Africa, it will still take you far. But at that stage I wouldn't say that I was particularly outstanding because there were so many talented sportsmen around, although I do remember getting Sportsman of the Year for the Under-13s!

I was just one of many kids who were good at sport at that age – I don't think I showed anything special in terms of potential. There is a huge pool of sporting talent at every age level in South Africa, encouraged by the sunshine, the huge amount of space and, if you were lucky like I was, excellent sporting facilities. We had superb facilities at school, acres and acres of rugby fields, in addition to athletics tracks and well-equipped gym halls – a great combination for a sports freak like me!

There are other, perhaps more fundamental, differences that I perceive between the schooling in South Africa and England, and one in particular appears to be a widespread lack of discipline in schools in the UK compared with those in South Africa. In South Africa we used to get caned even at the age of six and seven, and they really meant it when they beat us. It made us ensure that we were never naughty again, whatever we had done – not that I ever was!

When it came to any sport, competition was the buzzword at school as well as at home. All of my friends were talented on the sports field as well, but I had a will to win and a determination to beat them. They were much better than me to a man in the academic side of things, but when it came to sport it was a completely different matter. My best friends were Bruce Mussett, Brian Macauley, Jason Ferreira, Kerry Bosch and Johnny Henderson, all of whom I still see, and we were always trying to get one up on each other.

As a boy, my not unusual ambition was to be a Springbok rugby player. All white South African boys are brought up to believe that representing the Springboks is the ultimate achievement, and as I grew up the team was full of stars like Naas Botha, and the du Plessis brothers, Carel, Morné and Michael — my big sporting heroes who I was eager to emulate.

There was no thought then that I could play for England, why should there be? I did not think about that until three years ago, and even then I considered it the remotest of possibilities. At school a few people had told me that if I persevered I could be a Springbok later on, but I took it with a pinch of salt.

We did have a very good youth rugby team though, and we were unbeaten at Under-14 and Under-15 level. At Under-16s we lost a couple of games, something new to me at that stage! And then we had First and Second XVs, and began playing in some larger rugby competitions in which we always did well.

My first club league game was against Despatch and the legendary Danie Gerber was playing for them. He was playing at centre, and was then one of the heroes of the Springbok side. I was playing at full-back. The first time I got the ball I laid it off and he put me on the deck. He crushed me. I was only 18 years old and remember feeling terribly intimidated, and to make it much worse, we lost.

Intimidation is a big word in South African rugby, especially at club level. The opposition would typically come on and look for someone whom they could beat up, and mouth off to. It has actually been a very bad problem in South African sport, in every age group. It never used to be that physical at schoolboy level, but the verbal abuse we used to get on the field, from parents in particular, was unbelievable!

Because it was more verbal intimidation than physical, I never had any major injuries in my schooldays, although when I left school and began playing club rugby, I broke my arm, had six pins in my hand, an operation on my knee and broke my little finger all in quick succession. In the main, however, I just used to pull ligaments and sprain ankles because of the hard ground — nothing very serious. It was an advantage that I did gymnastics, which made me supple; I think it helped a lot.

On the rugby front all my early coaches were brilliant, as they were for athletics as well. Pat Clarke was my first-ever rugby coach, a 6ft 4ins Eastern Province player. He took us through Under-9 to Under-11 level and taught us the basics. Then we went on to be coached by Charlie Pautz, also very good and very competitive. He drummed the will to win into every one of us, although he needn't have worried. The players wanted success as much as he did.

Neil Thomson was my rugby coach in the first year at high school. He put me in the team as fly-half, arguing that I was too small to play flanker, which I was. I was happier after that, and it gave me more of a focus. It worked with our game plan as well. We had plenty of forwards who were bigger than me to fill those positions. It was the first turning-point in my rugby career in terms of the positional aspect of my play. He also made me vice-captain of his team, and we were unbeaten that year.

I left Grey High School in 1989 when I was 18 years old, and I tried to get into technikon, the equivalent of an English technical college. I did just four months studying mechanical engineering, and that was quite enough. I wasn't very good at it! By then I also had my mind on other things. I was playing reasonably good rugby and I had just broken into the Eastern Province senior side and could not really keep my brain focussed on mechanical engineering or college. I just wanted to train for rugby and concentrate on my triathlon – the most demanding of all sports when it comes to endurance.

The only reason I had gone to technikon was because I had received a sports bursary of R1,500 – about £300 at the time. I played rugby for them and also for the Crusaders club, a Port Elizabeth team. Later they merged with the technikon and it became known as Crusaders-Technikon.

After I bailed out of technikon I worked in Hasties Sports for six months, a sports shop down on the main road in Port Elizabeth. I was still living at home so I did not have many outgoings. I simply played rugby, and trained and competed at triathlon and athletics during the summer. It suited me well.

There was compulsory National Service in South Africa at the time but I slipped through the net thanks to rugby. I still have a vivid memory of the day my oldest brother, Douglas, went into the army, and we saw all the new recruits lining up in their brown uniforms. He was just 19 when he went in, and we were very worried as it was bad news up on the Angola borders where he was due to be posted. There were thousands and thousands of people milling around, and mum, Richard and myself were crying our eyes out.

Both of my two older brothers did National Service and Richard, my younger brother, did too, but one way or another I managed to avoid the draft. I wanted to get National Service out of the way when I left school, but two weeks before I was due to go into the forces I broke my arm playing rugby and they would not take me. In the end I was never drafted, as National Service became voluntary.

Instead, I worked for a while for my dad who has a big electrical company in Port Elizabeth, and manufactures house alarms. We had a family friend called Peter Sharman who lived in Jeffrey's Bay, a holiday resort area about 45 minutes from Port Elizabeth. He was into alarms as well, and used to buy them from my dad and install them locally. I helped with the installations in the Bay, and soon I went down and lived with him. Peter's company was called Coastal Security, and I was getting R600 a month, then about £120, on which I could live fairly well. It paid for the beers anyway!

Jeffrey's Bay is a wonderful place, and one of the best surfing spots in the whole world. There is another beautiful resort about 15 minutes away from Jeffrey's Bay called St Francis Bay, which is where my oldest brother, Douglas, lives now. Ironically, he has purchased a share in Peter Sharman's security company and business is thriving — despite not having my services as a quality fitter!

While I was working for Peter, I made my first big breakthrough in rugby. I came on as a reserve for the Eastern Province senior side against the Western Transvaal in the Currie Cup, my EP debut, on 4 August 1990, at the tender age of 18. I came on at centre to replace Springbok Michael du Plessis for the last five minutes of the game. To say I was excited is an understatement.

The game was at Olen Park in Western Transvaal in the heart of Millie Land, the corn veldt. The ground was really hard and dry, and it was also at altitude. They had rickety old wooden stands in the stadium and the place was full of farmers, as it's a huge farming community. They were all drinking and eating boerewors rolls — huge sausages that they used to braai or barbecue out in the carpark. It was a memorable occasion, and we won fairly convincingly. I touched the ball twice, and off we went, so I was quite happy!

It was unusual for an 18-year-old to be playing for the EP senior side then, as it was such a tremendously physical game. These days it's a little bit different. Now you're getting more 19- and 20-year-olds breaking through, but then I remember finding it tough, a real man's game, and genuinely hard for a green school-leaver.

Afterwards, I got chosen for the EP seven-a-side tournament up in Durban and we got through to the semi-final. They were the only other games I played for Eastern Province at that time.

I was working quite hard, and training with the EP squad four nights a week. It meant that I used to have to travel in from Jeffrey's Bay every Monday, Tuesday, Wednesday and Thursday. Monday used to be a lot of fitness training, Tuesday and Wednesday would be skills, and Thursday a team run-out. It was all very physical, especially for an 11-stone teenager. But, it kept me out of trouble and taught me self-defence — how not to take on the big boys! It certainly made me think twice about the physical requirements of the game, and encouraged me to go into the gym and work on the things that would develop my strength. I was not very quick at that stage, and began to work on my speed, too, so for several different reasons the EP experience was very fruitful.

I played five games in all for Eastern Province before I came over to England. I was dropped after the fifth game because I did not 'fit in with their strategy'. The initial game plan had been to run the ball, but it didn't work, so the captain told me to kick. Sadly, things didn't improve. As a result Eastern Province dropped me just because I did not suit their 'style of play', whatever that meant. The fact that I wasn't an Afrikaner also didn't help my cause. Around 90 per cent of the players in the EP side then were Afrikaners, and it was quite a thing for an 'Englishman' to break into the team. If anything, I was a bit of an outsider, and I was considered as one which made me feel somewhat uncomfortable. Coming from an 'English' school I could understand Afrikaans, but I couldn't really speak it very well, and I didn't have the confidence to join in with the conversation. I just kept quiet and got on with it, while they used to take the mickey out of me. They used to call me 'soutpil', or sometimes 'rooinek'. They call you 'soutpil' if you have one foot in South Africa and one foot in the UK, with your dick hanging in the sea – literally it means 'salty dick'. 'Rooi' means red. The nickname 'rooinek' is given to all the Englishmen who visit South Africa and burn their necks in the sun! It was all new to me, and with the difficulty I had communicating with the rest of the side it was very hard.

When I was dropped, I felt that it was my chance gone. It was the first time I had ever been dropped – other than when I was playing Under-10s and my best mate, Brian Macauley, got chosen ahead of me at full-back. I was devastated then, and even more so when EP dropped me. My confidence was shattered and went one way, down, but luckily my family pulled me through and somehow kept me training.

The local press made it into a big story, but not because of me personally. I was just another EP reject that season, another fly-half who bit the dust. If the team didn't win, they dropped players. I was the fourth fly-half to lose his place that year, and it was particularly disappointing for me because it was just before EP were going to play against Australia, a dream fixture if ever there was one. One of my younger brother's friends, Greg Miller, took my place. He used to play fly-half at school when I was playing full-back. At least when I got dropped from the Eastern Province team it was near the end of the season, which made it a little more bearable.

My English adventure really started on my twenty-first birthday. I remember it well, despite the drink! We had an aeroplane party where each room was designated as a different country, full of the food and drink associated with it – mainly drink, it has to be said! We started off in France where we had Champagne, and then we moved to Moscow for some vodka. We had a Mexican room full of tequila, and finally we ended up in South Africa for Castle beers, braaivleis, and biltong; it was a brilliant night!

Halfway through, in Moscow or Mexico, I can't remember which, the phone went and it was my brother, Peter, ringing from my Uncle Doug's house in Stroud. Some weeks earlier, my brother had been chosen for the South African triathlon team to go to the World Championships in Canada, and on the way back after the championships (he had come thirteenth in his age group), he went to England to visit my grandparents and uncle.

He wished me a happy birthday and said that I should come over to England because it was such good fun. Normally I would have said 'Yes I'll come,' and would have done nothing. But on the following Monday I was with my girlfriend, Carmen Rumsey, and I decided that I ought to grasp the opportunity and go. I didn't tell anyone other than Carmen until two days before I was due to leave. Within a week the travel agent had organised my flight and everything else I needed, including a visa.

I booked a return ticket, of course. As far as I was concerned it was simply an extended holiday to see my brother, far-flung family, and England – leaving Port Elizabeth was not on the agenda. I was also on a South African passport, with a limited duration visa, so I had to come home. My British passport came later.

When I told my mum she was very excited. Dad was a bit surprised because I was leaving my job, but there was nothing he could do about it, and he wasn't going to say no.

Even though I only planned to go abroad for a few months the boys gave me a very liquid farewell party before I left, and we really overdid the gargling!

The plan was that I would fly from Port Elizabeth to Johannesburg, stay in Johannesburg for two hours, and then catch my flight to Heathrow. I did that with some aplomb, but I had been so drunk that I did not pack my bag properly and I left all my addresses and telephone numbers at home, as well as all the details of where I had to go and who I had to contact when I got to the UK!

When I arrived at Heathrow I became a little lost South African boy a long way from home, out in the big wide world. Nobody wanted to help me, or that's how it felt. I didn't know where to go, or what to do. Eventually, I found Information but they couldn't help, and at that stage I just wanted to put my bags down and cry.

It had been a 13-hour flight so I had slept off the effects of the alcohol, although a few stiff drinks at that moment might have helped! I did not know where on earth my grandparents lived, nor my uncle and brother. I didn't know anything. All I could remember was that my mother had said that gran lived towards Gatwick Airport, so I hopped on a train heading in roughly the right direction. The problem was that I still didn't know where to go next. I strolled around for a while near the airport and finally booked in to a nearby bed and breakfast and sat in my room all night, depressed and in a state of panic. I had to find where my gran lived somehow, so I collected together all the 50p's I had and marched off to the telephone box (you have to remember the currency was new to me as well) desperate to try and get hold of my mother for all the names, numbers and addresses I had forgotten. You can imagine what she said to me when I finally got through!

My gran came and picked me up from Gatwick the next morning – which was a great relief. It turned out they were living just outside Eastbourne, so I had been heading the right way, and I stayed with them for a week. Despite being in their eighties they were still very mobile, and my gran used to organise everything to try and keep me entertained; in fact she really went to town. Gran is very 'into' antiques, castles, ghosts, and things like that, and she used to take me sightseeing, but the attraction of being a tourist soon wore off. By the time a week was up, I thought this is not for me, and so I set off for my Uncle Doug's in Stroud.

It was my first time there, and I was really pleased to see Peter again after so long. My uncle had a girlfriend, Cathy, and two daughters at home with him, and Peter had already discreetly warned me that it was openly 'very affectionate' in the house — something we were not really used to at home in Port Elizabeth.

I remember when I first walked in through the door and met 'the family'. Despite being 18 or 19 years old the two girls were complete strangers to Mike Catt from Port Elizabeth. But they were still keen to give me a kiss even before they said hello and introduced themselves. I was genuinely taken aback. It wouldn't have happened back in conservative South Africa I thought! Not even a shake of the hand and a polite greeting, just a straight kiss. I had definitely arrived in England!

Touching Down in Bath

Once I had settled in at home with my uncle, I began to start training again with Peter.

We used to run up and down the big hills in Stroud and, as a serious and talented triathlete, Peter also used to ride his bicycle in the mornings. Rain or shine we were up at 6 a.m. every day to train, and during the rest of the day we'd alternate between sleeping and eating all the food in the house!

Then, one day, my uncle had a day's holiday, and he began encouraging me to do something to alleviate my boredom. I did not have any friends in the area, and I didn't want to go sightseeing, but he told me that I couldn't sit around the house all day with a long face. In truth, I was very homesick, despite being with my brother. Most of all I was missing my close mates who had always been around. Suddenly they were not there, and I was in a strange and new environment. That was brought into sharp focus the first time I went out for an evening in Stroud. I visited a nightclub called Egypt Mill and was lucky not to be beaten up. It made my homesickness worse, and I began to think that England was not for me, particularly as that sort of thing didn't really ever happen in South Africa. It dawned on me how completely different the two countries are, and how the English culture was totally alien to me.

In November 1992, Uncle Doug decided to take matters into his own hands and look in the Yellow Pages to find a rugby club I could play for. I suppose he thought that the promise of a game of rugby would be one of the few things that would get me out of the house and put a smile back on my face!

We talked about playing for Sevenoaks, a Kent first-division side where my uncle used to play, but it was a bit too far to travel. The local club in Stroud also came up in conversation but Uncle Doug knew that I had played for Eastern Province, and said that playing for either of these sides wouldn't be challenging enough. Then he suggested giving one of the big teams a call, and Gloucester immediately sprang to mind because it's only 20 minutes away. First he called Directory Inquiries for the number, and events began to take their course. Uncle Doug gave the club a ring, but didn't get any answer. To this day, I don't know if it was the right telephone number he rang, or a wrong number, but we didn't have any luck, and in the end we tried Bath instead! Looking back on it now, I would probably have been back in South Africa long ago if I'd gone to play for Gloucester.

When the phone started ringing Uncle Doug passed the receiver to me. Initially I spoke to the secretary at Bath, a lady at the time, and she suggested that I should phone Gareth Chilcott at home. I had never heard of Bath Rugby Club, and I certainly hadn't heard of Gareth, even though he was such a huge character in English rugby. In the end I plucked up the courage to phone 'Cooch'. When I eventually got through he was seemingly very interested and he asked me more about myself, what positions I had played in when I was at home in South Africa, and at what levels. After I had filled him in with a potted life history he invited me down to train with the club, and it made me feel good. For the first time in a long while I felt that somebody wanted me for my rugby – or was at least interested in seeing what I could do. Cooch was very positive, and he said it would be 'brilliant to have me'. So, despite everything, I went training that Wednesday.

I remember being very scared to make that initial phone call. It was my uncle who pushed me all the way; then he made me go and have a look at the club to see what it was like. The spirit must have moved him, because it proved to be the start of my rapid progression in the English game and, as things have turned out, I have a lot to thank him for!

I got a lift down to my first training session at Lambridge, just off the A46. It was a 40-minute drive, and even as we drove down I was not sure about whether I wanted to go or not. I knew nothing at all about the club and when I arrived at the training session, I was very shy. I changed into the only rugby kit I had with me, my EP gear. I had brought an EP jersey over with me from South Africa, but had to go and buy myself a pair of boots from the local sports shop in Stroud to go to the training session. I must have looked like the new boy at school in my black-and-red striped kit, and my shiny boots.

Stuart Barnes was practising his kicking, and I recall him kicking a ball through the posts which then bounced and landed in the carpark. I went and picked the ball up, and kicked it back — very politely. He still says that I kicked it about 60 metres past him, but at the time he looked at me as if to say: 'Who the hell is this bloke in an Eastern Province kit?'

I was introduced to Cooch and to Brian Ashton, and they invited me to have a warm-up with the team. Together with Gareth, there were characters like Nigel Redmond, Ben Clarke, Richard Hill, Stuart Barnes, Jeremy Guscott, Phil de Glanville, Tony Swift, and Jon Webb at the training session, and it dawned on me how big a club Bath must be in the domestic English game. I had recently seen most of these players on the television watching the Five Nations highlights back in South Africa, and all of a sudden here I was on the same rugby field as them! I really couldn't believe it.

The first player I really met was Sean O'Leary, a lock. Sean was a towering 6ft 7ins and he came across and introduced himself while we were running round the pitch, and we chatted. I do not think Sean understood a word I said because of my clipped South African accent, which was much broader than it is now. But speaking to someone friendly helped put me at ease a little.

I warmed up with the first team for a while and did some ball skills, before Gareth asked me to go and continue training with the Second and Third XV team players on the other pitch. At the end of the session, the Third XV Spartans' captain, Clive Book, told me that I would be playing for them at number 10 against Plymouth Albion that weekend. I was in!

I had enjoyed the training session itself after having done nothing competitive for so long, and immediately began looking forward to the match on Saturday. Getting out there and playing again felt fantastic, and I realised how much I had missed it.

Brian Ashton later said that I was being eyed up straight away. 'Mike struck everyone as being quality material,' he told a newspaper reporter, but he didn't tell me on that first night.

I played for the thirds on the Saturday. The changing-room banter was an experience I wasn't used to. I had never met my scrum-half before, and after he introduced himself, he revealed that if he couldn't pass me the ball for one reason or another, he might just kick it to me, and was that okay. 'Don't stand too far away!' he added. It was all a good laugh, although it was still surprisingly competitive when you got on the field. I played quite well. I was also goal kicking that day and I kicked a couple of goals and conversions as we won without a problem. Afterwards I had a drink in the bar with my uncle who had come down to watch.

The next week I impressed again, and to my surprise I got a couple of write-ups in the rugby-mad local Bath paper: 'Spartans and the South African lad', was the headline, I remember. After that it didn't take long for me to be chosen for the second team, where I played just the one game at full-back. We lost and I ended up moving position to play at fly-half! That team included Ian Sanders, Steve Knight and Iestyn Lewis, who I got to know quite well. Iestyn was one of the first real friends I made in the club.

After two or three weeks travelling in from Stroud to Bath, I decided I was going to play for the club for a little bit longer at least, so I thought that I might as well rent a place in the city. I still had no intention of staying in the UK, I only had a four-month visa after all, but I felt it would be much easier to be close to the rugby club.

My plan was to rent a flat somewhere in Bath, but when I arrived I found a local youth hostel which was close to the rugby ground, and as I had a youth-hostel card — and was not flush with money — I went and stayed there for two weeks, living out of my rucksack.

It was always intended that my friend, Kerry Bosch, and girlfriend, Carmen, were going to come over and stay with me, and they were due to arrive at the end of that time. My intention was to rent a two-bedroom place for the three of us to live in, so, in the end, that's what I went in search of. I rented my first flat in Bath for £390 per month, just along the London Road near the training ground as you enter the city. Initially I thought it was fairly cheap. But then I realised I was still thinking in Rand — and R390 is pretty cheap. I hadn't converted it into sterling, and when I realised what I had done I felt a real idiot! The saving grace, I thought to myself, was that Carmen and Kerry would be sharing the costs with me. That was until neither of them came over.

I rented that place for three months, paying out £390 a month, with no job or other income to pay the bills. What's more, I didn't have any friends in the city, and I hardly knew anybody. I was becoming sad and lonely! The only thing I had was my rugby, so it's no wonder I used to get homesick.

But I did begin to feel increasingly comfortable in the Bath rugby set-up. I used to train regularly and go up to Bath University to work on my fitness. It was there that I really got to know some of the personalities in the Bath set-up — people like Ged Roddy and Iestyn. Another, Simon Johnson, used to live in Box, a small village near Bath, and he generally picked me up as it was on his way into the university. Iestyn was then in the Welsh Under-21 squad, and, like me, he was keen on his training. Being South African and Welsh, we could understand each other, even if nobody else could!

I had little else to do during the days as I wasn't working, so I tended to fall in with them and train hard. I got to know them all fairly well, and quickly too. They used to go up to the campus at 7 a.m. for an early-morning training session and stay up there after breakfast to watch videos of recent Bath and England games. Dedication or what! I also used to watch a couple of other games during the day. To all intents and purposes it was becoming a home away from home, as we lived up there most of the time.

However, I was running short of money. I had saved quite a lot of cash up until I was 21, and my grandparents had given me some money as well, but it was all going very quickly – especially as I went to Lanzarote on tour with the boys in December 1992. I was intending to go home to South Africa at the end of February, so there was still another two months for me to stretch out the cash, and the possibility of not being able to do so was causing me some concern.

The Lanzarote tour turned out to be a great holiday. I pulled my hamstring on the second day so I just had to sit in the sun. It was like being back at home. The weather was superb, and I really enjoyed relaxing and drinking beers by the pool all day. Even after we returned I couldn't play for a while but I got a lot of good treatment from the club and I was soon able to get back into the swing of things again.

Before setting off for the sun, sea and sand in Lanzarote I had made my first team début for Bath against Nottingham, at Nottingham, on 5 December 1992. It was a friendly and we won 24–17. However, the first senior match I really remember playing an active rôle in took place straight after I recovered from my injury, towards the end of January in 1993. It was a friendly at the Rec against London Irish and I played at fly-half. London Irish had Simon Geoghegan playing on the wing but we still won convincingly, 47–5, and I scored twice. It was a great thrill, and gave me all the extra confidence I needed at the time. It also renewed my determination to go further, and encouraged me to train even harder. People say that South Africans are arrogant, and I believe that's generally a good quality in a sportsman. I can be a bit arrogant on the rugby field, and I'm certainly determined, but you still need a confidence booster every now and again – and for me, that début home game against London Irish was the spur I needed.

After I played in the friendly against London Irish, Stuart Barnes returned to the Bath team, so myself and Iestyn Lewis, who also played in that game, dropped back down to the seconds for a short while. We didn't mind too much as we had such a successful Second XV, full of talented players like Steve Ojomoh, John Mallett, Gareth Adams and Audley Lumsden, who have now broken through at club and international level.

Three weeks later I made my Courage League début against Gloucester, again playing at fly-half. Jon Webb kicked five penalties for us and we won 20–0. Being a league game it was my big breakthrough into the Bath team at senior level. Although I gave a fairly good performance, it was not a good team effort and I remember Jack Rowell dishing it out in the changing-room afterwards. He gave the team a right bollocking, then turned round and praised me and Ian Sanders, the two new boys.

Around this time I discovered that 'initiation ceremonies' are much friendlier in England than they are in South Africa; the one at Bath is anyway!

We had a First XV initiation ceremony at Grey High School called 'Legs'. You had your tracksuit trousers around your ankles, and with your hands on your head and the captain holding the back of your pants, you had to walk through a line of the other boys while they whacked you on the legs! You used to have to go the whole distance with these boys slapping you really hard.

I did 'Legs' on my first school tour to Johannesburg after my début first-team appearance at full-back. The trouble was that I did not have big legs at the time, I still haven't, and I was bruised for days!

Playing for Eastern Province you would have to tell a three-second joke in Afrikaans standing on a chair. If you couldn't do it, you had to bend over a table while all the other players took turns whacking your backside. On top of that baptism of fire they made you sing the National Anthem in Afrikaans, and talk to them in their own tongue. If you got anything wrong you went through the beating procedure again.

It was all in stark contrast to the ceremony at Bath, which for me took place on my first away trip and involved rather a large number of rum coolers. I remember being dreadfully sick all over the bus after a considerable amount of rum and lager. We also had to stop off at a pub and sing songs. It was a much more 'gentlemanly' kind of initiation, which somehow highlights the two different ways of life. In South Africa you are often more scared of getting initiated than playing the game. In England you would rather get initiated than play!

I was already finding that training in the UK was very different to the training at home. In South Africa, our training on Mondays was solely fitness-oriented. You run, and run, and run, and that's all you do for the night, apart from chasing up and down steps. It's really draining. At Bath, on the other hand, you might have a 30-minute fitness session or run around, and then you get into ball handling and skills.

The official Bath training sessions were, and still are, on Monday and Wednesday evenings, but at that time I was up at the university virtually every day on the weights, and doing speed work and plyometrics with Ged Roddy and the boys. In South Africa they had not even heard of plyometrics, a training science which emphasises explosive running drills (bounding over hurdles for example) with the aim of increasing your speeds. In South Africa it's all about slogging away because you 'have to be match fit'.

In Bath I found a great deal more professionalism, both in coaching and playing terms. But the major advantage for me was that everybody spoke English! In a typical South African team it's a melting pot of blacks, coloureds, and Afrikaners. When you bring a provincial team together in South Africa it's very difficult to build a team spirit as they all speak different languages; the communication gap is a big divide. At least in Bath I could understand what the hell was going on.

Another of the main differences in the game here – something that took me by surprise when I started playing in England – is that all the forwards can handle the ball. They are not the biggest people, but they can all play with the ball a bit, whereas in South Africa we only had 20-stone louts. They were usually big hulking Afrikaners, only able to scrummage and fight and, to be honest, that's all they appeared to be there for. They didn't know how to catch a ball, and didn't seem to mind; all they wanted to do was scrummage and beat up opponents.

It was such a pleasure to see forwards passing the ball in my early days at Bath. I was amazed. You could base your game around it, which is just what Bath were doing, and still do. Indeed, I think that is why Bath have been so good for so long. Back in Port Elizabeth you would never get a forward standing in the back line, because he would either drop the ball or not be able to pass it. Give the ball to Ben Clarke or Steve Ojomoh and it becomes immediately apparent that they have good enough hands to pass the ball on. It's therefore a completely different game in England, and, for me, more enjoyable as a result.

In South Africa it was win at all costs. How you played did not matter, nor did kicking the hell out of the opposition, as long as you scored more points than them. There was no room for failure, and it was not for the squeamish. There was also no room for losers.

South Africa has a vast rugby playing population, with talent in abundance. There are a large number of players in South Africa to choose from who are able to play at international level. There must be 80 to 100 players who could be selected for the Springboks, and I believe that has ultimately given them a difficult selection problem. Too many talented players competing for too few places is also a problem which is evident at provincial level. There are so many options that players are continually being discarded, and in many cases it has been the players with the greatest potential who have been thrown out. The turnover in players is extraordinary, and they rarely give the most talented players time to grow into their positions. I think this has been the major pitfall of South African rugby since they have come out of sporting isolation. The team has been changed so many times, and it has played too many games and toured too much. In addition, the Springboks have also frequently changed their management. They have tried new coaches and managers, and have not been able to get the right team on or off the field, or stick with the same one for a significant period of time. There has been no continuity, which is so important when you are building a winning XV.

Again, in the UK, it's different. In England you have a select group of about 25 people who are good enough to play rugby at international level, and the management has stuck with them and built a squad. One only has to look at the change in fortune of the England side in the last five seasons to see the validity of this approach.

By mid-February 1993 Jack Rowell had seen me play a few times, despite the fact that it was still only my first season with Bath, and he mentioned in passing that there was a possibility that I could make the England Under-21 team, and even the tour of Australia in May. It was a classic Jack Rowell ploy. I had been all ready to go back to the Eastern Cape sunshine, but the promise of a representative tour was enough to make me reconsider. It was the key factor in my decision to stay in the UK. I am sure any aspiring rugby player would have done the same as I did, and stuck around.

I thought to myself, I can't play for England, can I? However, not once did it cross my mind that I could be on the way to a full England cap. I just thought there was a chance that I could play at England Under-21 level, and afterwards return to Port Elizabeth and win back my place in the Eastern Province side. I still wanted to go back and prove to them that they should never have dropped me, and then go on and play for the Springboks!

My rugby had improved dramatically in Bath over those few short winter months, but I was more homesick than ever. My brother had gone back to South Africa, and I was now in the mood to go back too; I was miserable! I didn't even have my own telephone and had to walk about a mile to the nearest phone box to phone my parents. It was so expensive, especially as I was not working.

What money I had left was going quickly, and when my girlfriend, Carmen, failed one of her exams at university, it meant that she had to retake it again in February. In the end we both felt that there was no point in her coming over to England, after all I would be back soon!

THREE

First Steps for England

I was meant to go back to South Africa at the end of February 1993, but Jack Rowell had whetted my appetite, and I decided that I really wanted to stay and win selection for the England Under-21s against the French Armed Forces – a curtain raiser to the Pilkington Cup final at the beginning of May 1993.

Before I had even left South Africa my dad, Jimmy, was already in the process of organising a British passport for me. I wanted one, not to stay in the UK as such, but because it would make travelling a lot easier. Travelling the world with a South African passport generally requires protracted applications for visas which is all very time consuming, and as I had an opportunity to have a British passport it seemed like a good idea. My dad got everything organised for me, and I finally received my British passport at the beginning of 1993. It was just as well!

I was thrilled to be selected for the game against the French at Twickenham – it was a dream come true. It was such an honour to play for the England Under-21s. I knew that I would never have been given that sort of opportunity in South Africa, which did not even have an Under-21 side when I was playing at that age level.

It was the first time that I had ever played at Twickenham and it was an awesome occasion, although there was only a small crowd as the match was staged as the lunchtime entertainment before the cup final. I had seen Twickenham on television in the past, but had never thought in my wildest dreams that I would ever play there. But all of a sudden, there I was, at only 21 years old.

The match kicked off at twelve o'clock, and while everybody else was in the carpark having a few drinks before the big game of the day, we were slaving away in a battle royale on the pitch. I played in the centre, and was also goalkicker.

My first two kicks were shocking (a bit like my full England début a little later) and they went nowhere near the posts. However, by the end of the game I had scored 21 points, including a try. I remember that try as if I had scored it yesterday. I was going to take a penalty, and the French were walking back. I decided to tap it and go when I spotted a bit of an opening, and ran between two forwards to score. There was a small round of applause, but no wild cheering. By then there were probably 10,000 people watching, but it didn't sound like it — it sounded to me like there were only one or two people there to see my magic moment but it didn't matter, I was thrilled.

I was very, very happy after that game, and I knew from then on that there was a good chance I would be chosen for the Australian tour at the end of May. The management seemed very impressed, and the papers had a bit of a field day with it as well: 'Catt Scores 21 Points' was one headline, 'Catt Gets the Cream' was another.

I was able to spend quite a lot of money on phone calls back to South Africa that night, because I had recently benefited from another stroke of good fortune. I had been introduced to west country entrepreneur Malcolm Pearce, and he took me on to work in one of his retail outlets, J.C.R. News, a smart newsagent in the High Street in Bath. It was another factor in my decision to stay on in England for a bit longer to see what would happen next. And what happened next was my formal inclusion in the Aussie tour party.

I booked a flight home for a holiday in South Africa in between the French game and the tour to Australia, purely to see my folks and catch up. When I went back for those three weeks everybody seemed amazed that I had done so much so quickly, and that I had already played for the England Under-21s. All of my family and friends wanted to know what it was like, and they were good enough not to tease me too much for being an English turncoat. When I left South Africa I had only just broken into the Eastern

Province team and, while I was known locally, nobody really knew of me in Durban or Johannesburg. It was probably a blessing in disguise, because when I went back on the full England tour to South Africa in 1994, I did not get any serious flak. Had I been a well-known player in South Africa before I left, and jumped ship to England, the crowds would certainly have let me know what they felt about it.

Back at home, sitting in the sun, with my creature comforts and my friends around me, it did cross my mind that I ought to stay in South Africa and forget England. But I had a job to go back to at the newsagents, a tour place booked to the other side of the world, and a new flat in Bath shared with some of my UK friends (later, it became affectionately known as the 'HIV flat'). So I had my three-week holiday in South Africa, and returned to the west country as I said I would.

It took me a while to adjust to living with John Mallett, Iestyn Lewis, Gareth Adams and Vicky Smith, but it turned out to be brilliant fun. I used to love staying in that flat. It was rugby, rugby, rugby, virtually all of the time, although a lot of things went on there which opened my innocent South African eyes to the big wide world!

On my return to the UK, the Under-21 squad only had time for a couple of training sessions up in Loughborough, and then we went straight off to Australia. The long flight over was an experience never to be forgotten! Some of the boys went on the beers, and prop Darren Crompton and I decided to join in, perhaps unwisely. We had our meal and then a few more beers, and by the time we were four or so hours out of Heathrow, they were running out of our favourite tipple on the aircraft. The assembled squad therefore decided to take matters into their own hands – literally – and began amusing themselves by stabbing neighbours with the plastic inflight cutlery, as only beered-up rugby players know how.

The airline duly ran out of beer, and so we turned to drinking vodka. By the time we got to Kuala Lumpur and had to change planes, most of us were very 'tired and emotional', and we were made to do a stretching session in the middle of the airport! There we were, giggling away, and much the worse for wear. We must have looked ridiculous bending and stretching in unison at the airport; around 26 of us swaying wildly about in our tracksuits, and providing the entertainment for international travellers from all parts of the world!

Yes, it was a fairly good trip on the way down under. It was a really good tour as well, and we played a Test Match against the Australian Under-21s as a curtain raiser for their senior side's game against South Africa in New South Wales.

They had a very good team but we were victorious. I scored a try from fly-half and converted all of the three tries we ran over, but I tore ligaments and nerves in my elbow and came off with ten minutes to go.

Kyran Bracken was playing in that match, and we became fairly good friends over the course of the last fortnight of the trip. He had arrived late on the tour because he had travelled with the England A team to Canada, and then returned to the UK to sit important exams. Consequently, Kyran could only come out to Australia for the last two weeks, but we roomed together after he arrived.

The journey back was as eventful and entertaining as the outward leg. A rugby tour of any sort must be an airline's worst nightmare. Mark Mapletoft passed out, so we decided it would be a good idea to cut his hair! He then proceeded to throw up over the seats of the aircraft when we had to get off at Kuala Lumpur. However, while most of the lads drunk themselves silly, Darren Crompton and myself were very quiet on the way home; we had learned our lesson . . . if only!

By the time we had returned to the UK I'd missed my own domestic season in South Africa. There was no point in going back, particularly as it would soon be the beginning of the 1993–94 English rugby season, which was full of promise. Another plus point for me was that I was also getting to see the world as a rugby player in England, and I was enjoying the new experience. In South Africa we are so isolated, and the only places we ever travelled to were Durban, Johannesburg and Cape Town. But already in the short time I had been in England, I had been to Lanzarote, Australia and back to South Africa, and I was down to go on the pre-season tour of Canada with Bath in August. I also felt my rugby was improving in leaps and bounds, and I was being given a chance in First XV games.

The three-week Canada tour in August provided another wonderful chance to travel, and was significant in that it proved to be a watershed in my rugby playing career with Bath. I had been playing at fly-half for the seconds, so when the club's usual fly-half Stuart Barnes decided not to go on the Canada tour, I knew it was a great opportunity for me to claim the regular fly-half role. I got my chance, and I believe it was in Canada that players like John Hall and Cooch began to think that I had some talent. I sensed that they were now considering me as part of their regular first-team squad, and I started to feel more comfortable about everything. I was at last getting to know all of the players, and becoming one of the team. On our return I soon got a longer run in the First XV at centre/fly-half, thanks to a combination of Phil de Glanville and Stuart Barnes being rested for international duty, and Jerry Guscott's well-documented long-term groin injury.

Things began to move quickly for me on the rugby field – even quicker than I had moved when I was doing the 'Legs' initiation ceremony. The New Zealand team toured England during November and December 1993, and I was chosen for the South West XV to play against New Zealand in Redruth – the game in which Phil de Glanville had his head stamped on. We lost, narrowly. I was chosen to play at fly-half, and looked on it as a rare opportunity to play against the best in the world. It was a superb experience. I played quite a good game, but it was badly disrupted when Phil was hurt. Having had what I thought was a 'rare opportunity' to play against the mighty All Blacks, I had a second chance to play against them almost immediately as I was selected to make my début for England A at Gateshead on 7 November. I played at centre, but not very well, and we were defeated 12–16. A fortnight later I notched up a hat-trick of games against the men in black when I played fly-half for the England Emerging XV against them at Gloucester. Again we lost, 19–32, playing against their mid-week side. I blamed the rain, but we did score a couple of good tries!

By then I had played with, or against, most of the other leading players who might have considered themselves as England hopefuls, and despite my dodgy performance for the A side, I had begun to think that I could go much further.

I was concentrating on playing at fly-half, so my rôle at centre for Bath – and for England A – was just a bonus: I was young and new to the side, and keen to play anywhere, an attitude which has generally stood me in good stead.

I was learning a lot from playing outside Stuart Barnes, a genius in his own way, and from playing for Bath, something I have always really enjoyed. I would even have played on the wing for the club if it had been required – the most important thing was being part of the team. We were winning every Saturday, and it's a big motivator. That period was a terrific learning curve for me.

I never would have believed anyone if they had said I would be competing against rugby players of such a high calibre at the age of 22. Sometimes I had to pinch myself to make sure it was real. I still do. It's difficult to believe what I have achieved over the last two and a half years.

I had finally broken through into the senior Bath side, and every time I filled in for Stuart Barnes, Jerry Guscott or Phil de Glanville I seemed to have a good game. I was taking my chances at the right time, and I was getting familiar with the top players and the many Bath internationals. It was exciting to be part of that clique, a remarkable pool of rugby talent.

While Jerry suffered with his long-term injury I became a regular, and we had a very good season losing only one game against Leicester. The success was like a drug. Once I had secured a proper place in the Bath First XV, I had an inkling that I might be able to get into the England set-up at some point in the future, but I did not believe there was any realistic chance for me until the 1995 World Cup was over.

When I played for England A against New Zealand I thought that it was as far as I was going to get for the time being. I was involved in some of the England squad sessions, when they took a squad of 30, but looked on it purely in terms of being a valuable experience.

There were hiccups along the way for me. The game we lost against Leicester in the 1993–94 season was the first defeat I had played in during my time with Bath, and it was an experience I hope I don't have too often. It was like a morgue in the dressing-room afterwards. Jack Rowell was not happy to lose one of the crunch games of the season, and defeat meant we had to perform brilliantly for the next couple of games.

Thinking back to just that one dressing-room scene, I can clearly see one of the reasons why the Bath team has been winning for so long; we hate defeat. Jack Rowell hates it, John Hall hates it, and Andy Robinson hates it, and that intensity of feeling invariably filters down to the new players, perhaps even frightening them into playing well.

More often than not, however, things went according to plan in that golden season. For instance, I remember playing against Will Carling for the first time in the 1994 Pilkington Cup semi-final against Harlequins. Barnesy passed me the ball and I skimmed past Will. It was a superb feeling and as I went past, I thought 'Yeees!!' He did eventually catch me by the finger, but by that time I had passed the ball on to Jon Callard and he had scored.

That was one of the best games I have ever played in. We won right at the end of the game, 26–25, with Tony Swift scoring the winner with two minutes to go. I sat on the team bus after that crunch match, and thought more about the Bath will to win. The fear of defeat is certainly one factor in the equation, but I think there is one other – experience, which Bath has had in abundance over the last ten years. For example, if we were ever losing, Andy Robinson would ask the referee how many minutes were left, and then pass on calm and reassuring instructions to his less than confident team-mates: 'Okay lads,' he would say, 'we still have eight minutes left. Relax and let it flow, let it happen.' He knew we could turn on the style if we wanted to.

By the end of the 1993–94 season I was one of the top try scorers for Bath, and I had been playing very well at centre in Jerry's absence. But I wasn't so arrogant as to think that I would be able to keep Jerry Guscott on the sidelines long-term; after all, he is the best centre in the world. With Barnsey still playing, and Phil de Glanville and Jerry Guscott as the established Bath centres, I would have been quite happy to play second-team rugby. As far as I was concerned, it was just a joy to be playing and winning. Winning is so important in sport, to any team, any player, and I'm no exception. When you are part of a winning team, you don't wake up on a Sunday morning with the storm clouds hanging over you. When I had been playing for Eastern Province we had been losing, and that was the reason the team was chopped and changed so much. Bath, on the other hand, nearly always won and our confidence was sky high. Winning encourages a settled team and a spirit of adventure, and means that you are always able to try new things on the field.

I had been playing very well, but I was not in the England squad for the first three Five Nations games in early 1994, and didn't expect to be. I was, therefore, very excited to be named as a replacement in the game against Wales, because Jerry Guscott was still injured, and Stuart Barnes preferred to go horse-racing at Cheltenham rather than sit on the bench (a well-reported story). Indeed, fate played a starring role in my entirely unexpected England début against Wales in the final Five Nations game; a début which lasted a comical and unforgettable three and a half minutes.

Wales had come to Twickenham determined to take the Grand Slam, but England were having none of it. I came on as a replacement at the end of the game, after Rob Andrew had to leave the field with a back injury. Rob suffered a knock and suddenly he could hardly walk. I didn't even see him go down. The next thing I remember was Geoff Cooke and the other boys on the bench shouting, 'Come on, Catty, get on, get on!'. It was a tense moment when I ran on to the pitch for the first time as a senior England rugby player, and incredibly it made me the fifth South African-born full-back to play for England, after Tuppy Owen-Smith, Hubert Freakes, Sydney Newman and Murray Hofmeyer.

It was a very busy and interesting three and a half minutes – and thankfully we were winning. Had we been losing it might have been a serious disaster. Wales had just scored, and we had a kick-off. Somebody had to take the drop-out in Rob's absence, and that somebody was me. Seconds after I ran on the pitch for my first full England cap, I had to take a kick. I held the ball in my shaking hands, and tried to stop my knees knocking. My mind went completely blank and I just couldn't think what to do, but I did know that I had to make a decent kick, come what may. Thankfully, it was alright, but I was so nervous I don't know how I did it. To be honest, I've never been so jittery, despite the encouragement from the team and the crowd.

Straightaway the Welsh put up a high kick from their own 22, and I was standing right under the ball on the halfway line. It was coming my way, dammit! With my heart in my mouth I began running to catch it, but instead I knocked the ball on. The crowd went 'Ooooo', like they do, and that made me even more nervous!

But the three and a half minutes of hell didn't end there. We won a penalty in the Welsh half, and Will Carling indicated that I should take the kick. I must have looked at him with a blank expression, because then he looked over at Ian Hunter. I thought that was it; Ian was going to take the kick, but then Will looked back at me again and asked me if I wanted to take it. Despite the shakes, I said yes, of course. I thought I might as well have a go for glory.

In front of 70,000 people at Twickenham, and with the rest of the world watching, I lined up to take the place kick, still trembling like a leaf. In my mind's eye, I had the technical manual open at the page about place kicking. I thought it through step by step, and went through the motions in my head; how I was going to kick the ball and where. I teed the ball up and tried to relax, breathing slowly, in and out. All I could see out of the corner of my eye was a line of white jerseys stretching out across the field, and the two poles. I was thinking positively; this ball is going right through the middle of the posts.

When I walked up and kicked the ball, I felt fine. The rhythm was perfect. I thought I'd stroked it quite well, and from where I was standing it looked like it was going right through the middle of the posts. Sadly, the elation was very brief, as the ball went nowhere near the goalposts! In fact, it must have taken a very big deviation, or hit a stiff wind in midair, because while it may have been straight it wasn't long – the ball just struggled, bobbled, over the 22-yard line. It was a feeble effort, woefully short. Had it been a drop-out or a kick-off it would have been perfect, because the forwards could have run and caught it. The crowd just went 'Oooo' again, but I think they understood. I had a bit of a chuckle to myself. What a start to international rugby!

I didn't get another touch, although somehow I managed a late tackle as the final whistle blew, and it ended in a bit of a scuffle with Neil Jenkins and Nigel Davies. I was glad the whistle had blown and the nightmare was over.

Not surprisingly, I got a bit of ribbing in the dressing-room before I met the President to receive my cap and tie. He came into the changing-room, shook my hand and gave me my full England cap. I was very proud. Then one of the players, Dewi, I think, started shouting 'ANC! ANC! ANC!' and the whole changing-room started to join in. It was all in fun, done with a smile, particularly as we had won.

I phoned my dad who had watched it live on television in South Africa, and he was chuffed. He always moans about my kicking anyway, and he told me I was 'kuk' – which is a South African way of saying that I was crap. But he was laughing at the time and he, too, was clearly very pleased, and proud. I spoke to my brothers as well before we went off to the Hilton Hotel for the post-match dinner. That night I ran up a £300 room bill phoning home to South Africa. But it was a great night and well worth it; it's a memory I'll cherish.

In terms of rugby I'm English now, but in reality I'm never likely to think of myself as a 'complete Englishman'. My heart is always going to be in South Africa, which is still home. My boyhood dream had been to play for the Springboks, and, in some respects, I feel it would still be wonderful to play for them. But I know it's never going to happen, and I'm thrilled with the opportunities that have come my way wearing the red rose of England, and how things have gone — so far.

After Bath's solitary defeat against Leicester the team got into the swing of things and remained unbeaten for the rest of the 1993–94 season. We won the Courage League when we took on Northampton at home, although I was injured and did not play. I had hurt my ankle in the cup semi-final against Harlequins in April, and torn ligaments. The injury was a scare because the England squad were touring South Africa in May 1994, and now I was in the frame for selection. There was a fight against time to see if I could get on the tour 'home' — the first chance for me to wear an England rose on my chest in South Africa. I desperately wanted to go; a free trip meant that I could see my folks and my friends. But more important, I wanted to be seen wearing that England rugby jersey.

Bath had just won the Courage League when it was announced that Jack Rowell was going to succeed Geoff Cooke as England's new manager and, therefore, would lead that tour to South Africa. A lot of the Bath team had guessed that he would get the job and they were very happy, and perhaps a little relieved, that he won the post. Jack's a Bath man through and through, and some of the up-and-coming players in the team must have hoped that the appointment would help them enhance their own international ambitions; after all, at that time Jack knew more about the talent in Bath than anywhere else. I certainly hoped it might help speed my international progress in the future, particularly as it had been Jack who had initially introduced me to the England set-up.

Because of injury, I missed out on the victory which clinched the Courage League – the first of many championships for me, I hope – and I still had a bad ankle from my first Pilkington Cup semi-final, although I played in the Cup final game against Leicester. Once again, there was a full house at Twickenham, featuring a world-record number of spectators watching a club match, and yet another showpiece final for Bath. I met Prince Edward, and later I rounded things off with a try. In fact, I scored the winning try with ten minutes of the second half to go, finishing a move in the right-hand corner having taken a spectacular pass from Jon 'J.C.' Callard.

As I turned around, I remember being acutely aware of a sea of blue, black and white flags and scarves – it was an incredible feeling. We won the game 21–9, with the cup victory notching up Bath's thirteenth honour (out of a possible eighteen on offer) since 1984.

I was on such a high. We had won the Pilkington Cup, and it was just the right way to end a perfect season, for the club and for me. It surely couldn't get any better.

FOUR

My First Tour Home

Although I was confident of being picked for the touring squad, it was still a great thrill to receive the confirmation that I had been chosen for the England tour of South Africa in July 1994. I knew, however, that for most of the key games I would be on the bench covering as a utility back. I was really excited about going home, and not at all disappointed that I would only get to play in mid-week games. I was more than happy to do so just for the experience. I had won my full England cap against Wales, and now had the chance to build on it and get a freebie trip home!

Before we left England, there had been some doubt as to whether the tour would go ahead because some commentators expected violence after the elections, which happily failed to materialise. But there was a bombing incident in Jan Smuts airport in Johannesburg about two weeks before we arrived, and that further unsettled one or two of the players, particularly my Bath team-mate, Victor Ubogu. The coloured England players in the squad were especially twitchy about the trip, anxious about the racism they had heard so much about, and the prospect of trouble. I tried to reassure them as best I could, arguing that it was not nearly as bad as they had read, and that they ought to go with an open mind. 'You'll see a complete change,' I told them. 'It's not how everybody makes it out to be. There are no killings on the street corners.'

Luckily, the tour went ahead and I was really glad it did. My dad and some friends were at the airport to meet us, and we had an excellent reception when we arrived in South Africa.

We stayed in Durban for the first week and, apart from the training, we had some time to relax. It would be true to say that our minds were not entirely focussed on the rugby to come, and mine least of all. I was so glad to be back home again – back with my family and friends.

The games we played were very, very hard, but we had expected nothing less. I had warned the England side from the beginning of the tour that the South African teams were going to be very physical, and that they were capable of giving us a lesson in commitment. But at least the opposition were not looking out for me in particular, as a South African traitor!

We lost the first game of the tour quite convincingly – 22–11 – playing against an aggressive and highly motivated Orange Free State XV at the Free State Stadium in Bloemfontein. It was a physical confrontation and I badly bruised my shoulder making a crashing tackle on Andre Venter. We fielded a young team which had never played together, certainly not in the kind of testing conditions we encountered. The Orange Free State team, on the other hand, had something of a reputation against touring sides, and gave us an uncomfortable afternoon.

Stuart Barnes made himself a bit unpopular in the Free State, to say the least, after we had an ice-cold 'welcome' at the reception following the defeat. Barnesy hit the front pages across the whole of South Africa after delivering a stinging criticism of the way we were treated in Bloemfontein, and the people involved. He was right, and I also got some stick for delivering a few well-chosen words in Afrikaans as we walked out!

The next fixture was against Natal in Durban that Saturday, one of the top provincial sides in South Africa. Though I was on the bench, and we lost again 21–6, it was a much more enjoyable occasion. Natal is like England. Everyone comes early and makes a day of it, with curtain raisers to the game starting at 10 a.m. After we had been to the post-match function, we went down to one of the carparks and met some locals for a beer or two and they were really hospitable, which gave the players a much better impression of the way most South Africans behave.

I was still carrying my shoulder injury as the week progressed, so I did not play on the Wednesday against Western Transvaal. Will Carling had to fill in for me, which was my claim to fame on the tour! In all, six of the side that played in the first Test in Pretoria were selected for this particular mid-week game as we needed a win to steady the ship after the two opening defeats. It was another fierce but entertaining game. We narrowly beat Western Transvaal 26–24 and it helped improve morale.

We played a couple more games before the first Test. The key match was against Transvaal at the superb Ellis Park in Johannesburg – one of the best rugby stadiums in the world and the venue for the 1995 World Cup final. It holds some 62,000 and really is a magnificent sight.

We were very clued up for that game and very keen to beat them. But the squad was already beginning to tire by then, largely because of the physical demands put on us by the size of our opponents. That afternoon, they seemed to have more commitment, more of a desire to win. It was as if we were just there to make up the numbers. Despite two tries from both sides, the balance of penalties favoured Transvaal and we were unable to resist the quality of their running rugby – we went down, 24–21.

This was followed by a mid-week match against South Africa A in Kimberley – a game we lost 19–16, but should have won. Here the refereeing was the main culprit, as it was appalling. It seemed to us that South African referees didn't know how to handle the games. They appeared to be biased throughout our tour, and often seemed to be out of their depth. The referees came in for a lot of stick, especially when it came to handling the frequent fighting on the field. The South Africans have been renowned for fighting and stamping over the years and, with their home-grown referees apparently choosing to ignore serious incidents on that tour, it did not surprise the England squad that trouble continued to erupt, but it certainly upset us.

The first Test in Pretoria was coming up the following weekend, and it was clearly going to be a big game. We knew that we would have to win the Test to make the tour a success. I was chosen to be on the bench, and we trained really hard all that week.

The tension was high before the game — I remember Dewi Morris being physically sick with nerves — and we were all really fired up. But once we got on the field, the tension vanished, and we annihilated the Springboks.

From start to finish, the day was superb. We met the past president F.W. De Klerk in the tunnel, and Nelson Mandela who was just in front of him. It was a great honour to meet President Mandela because he has done so much for my home country. Speaking as a native South African, I think he's done a remarkable job in continuing the process of bringing together the many parties that have been in opposition to one another for so long.

It was the first time I'd heard the new anthem and the band also played the Afrikaans anthem *Die Stem*, the national anthem of my childhood. They sang *Nkosi Sikelel' iAfrica* first and nobody really knew it, and then the band struck up *Die Stem*. Bearing in mind that the match was being played deep in farming country, the whole crowd began singing and it touched me deep inside, so much so that suddenly I started singing with them — even though I was wearing an England jersey!

The win in Pretoria was a really big relief for Jack Rowell as well as the players because it was his first tour as an England coach, and meant that he could now go back home with his head held high. It was also important for Will Carling who was being pushed for his place in the England side at the time, with some critics saying that he shouldn't be captain. There was a lot at stake, and the boys went out and gave a superb performance. Tim Rodber had an awesome game, and all of the back row played a blinder. Many people refer to it as Rob Andrew's game, although there have been so many of them! Throughout the game, Rob's kicking was faultless, and in addition he ran in a superb try to give himself a tally of 27 points in the match; not bad when one recalls the score — 32–15. But it took a lot out of the team who were now even more exhausted, and there was only a one-week break for us to recuperate before the second Test in Cape Town.

On the Sunday we had a really good barbecue, and that's where I think we went off the rails. For the most part, the hospitality from the people of South Africa was brilliant. They really know how to throw a party, and definitely know how to host touring sides. We fell for it!

En route to Cape Town for the second Test, we travelled to play Eastern Province, and this is where events took a turn for the worse. Port Elizabeth is my home town and I wanted everybody to like it, but the trip was a disaster and the players hated the place.

We had a shocking flight down because of the weather. To cap it all, when we arrived we went to the wrong hotel and it was still raining hard and the wind was howling. There was nothing to do — there isn't much in Port Elizabeth except the lovely beach front, but that's no good if it's raining. By the time we got to the Holiday Inn, the hotel we were booked into, the mood had taken a turn for the worse, and the team was not impressed with the facilities.

I was, nevertheless, really looking forward to playing against EP, not least because my younger brother, Richard, was going to be on the England bench! Dewi Morris had been injured in the first Test and we didn't want to risk him in advance of the second, so we desperately needed another scrum-half to sit on the bench as cover for Steve Bates, who was playing in place of Dewi. Jack Rowell asked me what position my brother played in, and I told him that Richard was a scrum-half. He then asked if he was any good. After a short conversation, and presumably on my recommendation, Richard was put on the England bench, rather than the management flying somebody else out to South Africa for just a few days. We had arranged that Steve would go off with about five minutes to go, so Richard could come on and play for England in his home town! We had to get clearance from the Eastern Province Rugby Union, which we did, and so my young brother got his England jersey. But, in the end, he didn't get to play as the match turned ugly.

It was the game in which Jon Callard was horrifically injured, and Tim Rodber, one of our heroes from the first Test Match, was sent off. It was the first time that an England player had been sent off for 19 years. The game was over-physical and violent throughout. Jon Callard had to have 25 stitches in his face after being stamped on by the EP lock, Van der Berg, and Tim Rodber got his marching orders for responding in kind to EP's Simon Tremain. So much for Port Elizabeth, once known as the 'friendly city'. Though we won the game 31–13, and Paul Hull scored two good tries, it was a very dirty encounter, and very upsetting for both of the boys from Port Elizabeth. It was as if someone had asked the EP team to do as much damage to the England team as they could prior to the second Test, which the Springboks had to win to level the two match series. The referee did nothing to help control the game; he was terrible, and somehow the touch-judges didn't see anything at all.

Despite it all I had a pretty good game. Jon Callard was off the field so I was kicking, and I did well. We also scored three tries, something we had failed to do on the tour. We had won the battle, but the memory of it is a painful one.

The England team went to the post-match function afterwards and walked in and walked out. That day, Eastern Province was not for us. Richard Catt may get another chance someday as he is coming to play for Bath next season!

I felt very bitter about the whole thing, especially as it all took place in my home town. I had so much wanted to show the team around, and show them the sights, but the trip to PE and the game itself had gone so badly that they just wanted to get out of there as soon as possible. I could hardly blame them.

Things improved marginally when we went down to Cape Town. We stayed in the Cape Sun, one of the most beautiful hotels on the Cape, but we could sense things were not quite right. Tim Rodber was depressed after being sent off, and he also had flu which didn't help. The training sessions weren't very good either, possibly due to the fact that we were physically and mentally spent – the first Test had done for us.

The second Test was the last game of the three-and-a-half-week trip. Overall, I don't think any one of us would have then considered it to have been a very good tour, although the record books would have argued differently had we won the Cape Town Test to win the series 2–0. As it was, we had only won a total of three matches coming into the final match.

Cape Town was wet and windy for the Test, which suited our game, or so we thought. But the South Africans came out with such venom and determination to win, that we knew almost from the beginning they were going to overpower us. It was very disappointing. We thought we had done well to keep the score down to 3–3 at half-time, but then they let loose and tiredness became a big factor – we'd just had enough. In the end the Springboks ran away with the game and we lost 9–27.

After the match, there was relief tinged with the bitter taste of defeat. Later on, however, we still found the energy to celebrate as Will announced he was getting married.

I was not particularly happy with my own contribution to the tour in playing terms. Mentally, I was nowhere, and it was made worse by the fact that I was back on home territory. It was so great to be back. Although I played steadily throughout, I think I could have done a lot better if I'd been more focussed.

I didn't feel as though my place in the squad was under threat as the team was playing fairly well and didn't have any other utility backs. Stuart Barnes was on the tour, but he was due to retire, and I therefore figured that I had a good chance of staying in the selection frame.

In a way, I suppose, the disappointments of the tour made us even more determined to do well in South Africa the next time we visited the country, for the World Cup. It certainly helped us acclimatise to the demands of South Africa – to get used to the heat and playing at altitude, as well as the physical demands of the game itself in the southern hemisphere.

When I had a bit more time to relax after the tour ended, I sat in the sun and thought about how things had changed so quickly for me, and so dramatically.

I believe I would have played for South Africa at some point if I had stayed at home and developed my rugby there, or if I had chosen not to play for England and gone back to Eastern Province; but *when* is another matter. Now I will never find out.

Had I milked the rich and rewarding experience of playing in the Bath set-up under Jack Rowell, and taken that knowledge back to South Africa, I might have broken through into the senior side sooner rather than later. But there is so much politics in Springbok rugby that it's impossible to say for sure.

I suspect that had I returned, I would still be waiting to make my South African début. Certainly I would not have made it to the top as quickly as I have done in the English game. For that and many other reasons, I have no regrets about staying in the northern hemisphere. I love playing for Bath and England.

I stayed in South Africa for a further four weeks after the England tour to see my family and friends, and flew back to the UK in August 1994, in time for the pre-season build-up. I didn't have to wait long to see the sun again as we went to Barbados for a memorable Bath RFC tour. I had just split up from my girlfriend, who had planned to come with me as wives and partners were invited, so I ended up travelling alone and rooming with Ed Rayner – a bit of a space cadet! Ed is from Oxford and is renowned in the club as a very, very intelligent guy. He plays at fly-half and centre. Intelligent he may be, but he used to wake up in the morning unable to find any of his clothes! He wouldn't know where he had put them – within days of the tour starting he'd lost his wallet, his watch, his shoes, his socks; everything. It was farcical, but a lot of fun.

We only played two games in Barbados and it proved the perfect place for some rest and recuperation. It also brought the Bath team back together in great spirits for what promised to be a difficult new season.

FIVE

Back in Bath for the New Season

The Bath team arrived back from Barbados and went almost straight into the 1994—95 season, with a game against the Barbarians.

As always, there were great expectations. Stuart Barnes and Richard Hill had retired, and myself and Ian Sanders were the players earmarked to fill their boots – an almost impossible task.

Many of the so-called experts had said that Bath were going to miss Barnes and Hill, that it was the end of an era, and that we were not going to be able to cope. Ian Sanders and I were determined to prove them all wrong. Yes, we were stepping in for top-class international players with a lot of experience, players who had done everything with Bath. But I had been playing alongside Stuart Barnes for some time and I felt confident that I would eventually be able to fill his rôle pretty handsomely.

However, there had been other changes at Bath RFC during the summer break apart from these two retirements, and when we came to start the 1994—95 season it looked like a completely different set-up. Gareth Chilcott had retired, so the Bath forwards had also undergone enforced changes. In addition, we also had a new coaching and management structure. We thought Brian Ashton was the ideal person to fill Jack Rowell's boots. He'd been around for some five years, seen players come and go, and was very well respected at Bath. He could also work well with our captain, John Hall.

In all respects it was the start of a new era for Bath as a club, but the expectations were, nevertheless, as high as ever. Every time Bath enter a new season, the supporters always look for you to win the league and the cup – they expect you to win the league and the cup, indeed every game – and most of the time Bath do not disappoint. But with the enforced changes this year, and a team full of internationals thinking dreamily of a trip to the World Cup, and representative honours, it was always going to be hard to deliver.

The first couple of games didn't go particularly well. I was still struggling to get into the number 10 position, mainly because I had been playing at centre for most of 1993–94. There were already a lot of people in the club bar who were saying the team was missing Stuart. I wasn't uncomfortable about moving to fly-half. Jon Callard was at full-back and there was therefore no chance for me to play at full-back. Jerry Guscott had returned to the side and rekindled his partnership with Phil de Glanville in the centre, and so it meant that fly-half was the only position I could really fill for the team, and I was happy to do so.

Those early games were very hard. Without the knowledge and experience of people like Jack Rowell in the background telling us what to do and how to do it, it was entirely down to the players to perform and succeed. I was among a number of players who felt that the training arrangements were not as good as when Jack had been there, although we all appreciated that Brian was doing the best he could.

I wasn't happy with my club game right up until Christmas. I'd done enough, but I felt that there was a lot more to come. Much of it was down to the way the whole team was playing, because we weren't getting enough ball. We were not winning our share of line-outs and, consequently, we were not getting much continuity. My game went out of the window as a result. I'm more of a runner than a kicker, so I was keen to get the flowing movements in, and it just wasn't happening.

Bath were still winning those early games but we weren't playing well, and there was a feeling in the dressing-room that perhaps we no longer had a fifth gear. In the past Bath could always find that extra gear, another dimension, when it got tight. But more and more we began to think it had gone into retirement, along with Barnes, Hill and Chilcott.

We also seemed to have lost the focus and the commitment which historically went hand in glove playing for Bath. The season was continually disrupted by international duty. Part of Bath's problem stemmed from the number of international games and the number of international players at the club. More blame, perhaps, can be laid at the feet of new England boss Jack Rowell who demands total dedication from his international squad. That was bound to have an impact on Bath as a club. In the past Jack ensured that we were entirely focussed on Bath success. Now Jack was demanding the same kind of blinkered commitment to the national team, and with so many players on England duty it meant that some effort and commitment had to be re-focussed away from the Bath domestic season.

In many ways Jack hijacked the commitment of his Bath internationals. It's unbelievable and I don't know how he did it, but he turned things round completely. This season it was not for Bath anymore — something which Jack had drummed into us for such a long time — it was for England.

At the beginning of the season Bath introduced a new playing rota system, and from the start I don't think it worked very well, another contributing factor to our lukewarm performances all year. Conscious that the season would be badly interrupted by preparations for the World Cup, the Five Nations Championship and the other internationals against Canada and Romania, the club felt that a system which gave senior players a breather every now and then would also provide a valuable opportunity for younger players to gain some first team experience. In some respects it was an idea worth trying out. But, looking back, it has just added to our list of problems. Jack used to pick the best side for every game, and if he thought somebody needed to be dropped, he would do it. With the new rota system, Brian has been trying to keep everybody happy and, while it is a laudable aim, it doesn't necessarily go hand in hand with producing quality rugby week in, week out. In the future I'd like to see the rota go. If you are there to play a season with Bath, you should play it in full, and if you don't perform you should be dropped to the second team. But during the 1994–95 season everybody was getting a game, and players were even being promised matches by members of the club with no official rôle in team selection, which didn't help. We weren't playing with the same team every Saturday and it added to the general disruption. As a result we failed to get into the rhythm and flow of things in the same way as we had done in the seasons before.

Nevertheless, it's not much of an excuse, as we still had some of the best players in the country playing for Bath, so it was our fault if we drew or lost; but, it has to be said, the World Cup and other representative honours were always in the back of our minds.

The Bath domestic season was interrupted early on by the England games against Romania and Canada at the end of 1994. I was put on the bench for the two internationals, covering for Rob Andrew and Paul Hull, and already I felt a conflict brewing between club and country. It was only after Christmas, however, that the Bath team started to feel it was going to be difficult winning the Courage League again.

There wasn't a particular game where it struck home, but when we drew away with Orrell 6–6, and with Leicester 20–20 at home at the Rec, our faces told the story of woe. We knew we should have won both of those games, and the one against Leicester in particular.

The draw against Orrell at Edge Hall Road in February really signalled the start of our downfall. It's always hard up there – we knew it would be, having been pushed very hard by Orrell in the fifth round of the Pilkington Cup just a month earlier. Then we ran out 25–19 winners. But in the league game we played badly. Bath did not produce the goods at all and, to be honest, we were pathetic.

In March we drew 19–19 with Gloucester at home, and if there was any game that can be described as a turning point, that was it. I remember someone saying: 'We don't draw at the Rec, we don't lose at the Rec.' A draw like that was considered to be as bad as a defeat, and even then we only just pulled that out of the bag in the last few minutes. It was so disappointing, because we know that we are capable of playing top-quality rugby. We knew we should have won.

It was another very poor performance, a shocking display. Bath sat back and let Gloucester play well, and we watched them do it. We were playing catch-up rugby all the time. Luckily, I made a telling little break down the midfield with five minutes to go, probably the best thing I did in the whole game, and Jon Callard finished off the move underneath the posts. It was just as well because we were 19–12 down at that stage. J.C. converted the try to bring the final score level at 19–19. When we got in the changing-room it was deadly quiet.

I don't believe the Bath crowds saw us play a decent game of league rugby all season, until we beat West Hartlepool 53–17 in April. We played well in that one league fixture, and ironically a lot of the England players did not play, including myself! The team felt that there had to be at least one game where everything clicked together as we had planned, but it never happened until that West Hartlepool match. In the final analysis, it was only one of three games this season in which we performed well – the other two were the Pilkington Cup semi-final and final.

Our game has been stop-start-stop-start all year. Skipper John Hall has done his best to get us going – he has been the one shouting encouragement and advice, trying to put things right – but this year commitment to the club has taken a back seat. That will have to change next season.

The Hong Kong Sevens also caused a few problems this year, particularly the participation of Victor Ubogu. Jerry Guscott had informed the club that he would be going to Hong Kong well before the beginning of the season, which everybody felt was fair enough. Victor, on the other hand, left it right to the very last moment to say that he was going to the tournament. That attitude went down badly with the team and the management, and he was given a hard time. Victor knew he was going to get some grief when he got back, especially as Bath lost against Wasps while he was away. He must have felt terribly guilty.

I think that one or two of the boys actually went about castigating him in the wrong way. The debate should have been internalised and not held in the press and on television. But feelings were running high. I'm sure that had Jack Rowell still been in charge at the Rec he would have dropped Victor! The team itself gave him a bit of abuse, but in instances like that you have to try and put the squabbles behind you and get on with things.

Losing to Wasps away at the end of March was a crucial game for us. It was the first time we had lost for ages. Wasps were in third place when we lost to them at Sudbury, while Leicester beat West Hartlepool 12–6 at Brierton Lane on the same afternoon, thanks to the trusty boot of Jez Harris. We were brought down to earth with a bump. Wasps showed more commitment, and in winning kept their hope of achieving the Courage title alive. In one fell swoop it made the championship a three-horse race and put the Tigers on top of the table on points difference. That hurt. All credit to Wasps though. They played well, and their ball retention was good, but we never got into the swing of things.

I played the game at centre, with Richard Butland at fly-half. In the first half we had played into a strong wind, and we were completely knocked out of our stride. Without Victor, Jerry Guscott, and John Hall, who was also absent, we struggled and were 11–0 down early into the second half. With the strengthening wind behind us after the turn, we tried to claw back the deficit – something that we have historically been good at! Jon Callard pulled back three points with a penalty and soon set up a Bath try in which I played a key rôle. After I had been tackled a metre short from the line, Richard Butland went over for the score and the game was back in the melting pot, 11–10 after the conversion. However, this time, we just couldn't come back.

Bath captain for the day Phil de Glanville blamed the unsettled nature of the side, and squarely pointed the finger at the missing Victor. 'The players feel let down,' he told the press. 'Players do not do that sort of thing at Bath,' he told Stephen Evans of the *Independent on Sunday*. Phil repeated as much in front of the *Rugby Special* cameras, frustratedly adding that the squad had been unable

At an early age I was used to picking up silverware — Grey Junior School, Sportsman of the Year, 1984

On tour with Grey High School in Cape Town, 1988. Once I saw the gap, I went for it!

Breaking free, I score a try against a strong Western Transvaal side on my début for Eastern Province Under-21s. Boet Erasmus Stadium, May 1990 (The Evening Post, *Port Elizabeth)*

Me with my Uncle Doug and his girlfriend, Cathy

As a native of South Africa, I was able to help some of my England tour party pals find their way to the top of Table Mountain, Cape Town

A proud moment as I am presented to the newly elected President of South Africa, Nelson Mandela, before the first Test between England and South Africa at Ellis Park, Johannesburg, during the 1994 tour

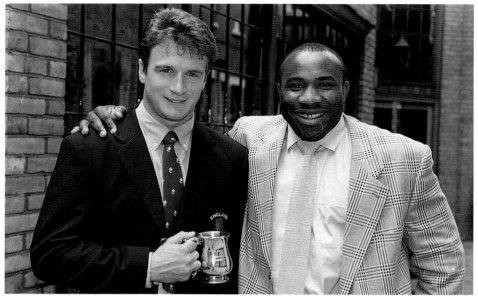

My Bath and England colleague, Victor Ubogu, congratulates me on winning the Whitbread Flowers Rugby World Award for the Most Promising Player of 1995 (Colorsport)

England celebrating after the first Test match in South Africa, 1994!

'The Mizuno Boys' celebrate the 1995 Grand Slam

Me with the Calcutta Cup and the Five Nations Championship Trophy after the international against Scotland in March 1995

My World Cup trip begins — a hint of anxiety?! (South African Airways)

In the thick of the action: Bath v the Barbarians, 3 September 1994. The match, which Bath won 28–18, celebrated 100 years of playing rugby at Bath's Recreation Ground (The Bath Chronicle)

Running with the ball is an important aspect of my game at full-back. Here I'm looking to attack against Wales at Cardiff Arms Park, February 1995 (David Rogers, Allsport)

to get together after the Five Nations Championship until the Wednesday before the game at Sudbury. But, more than anything, I think our tactical planning may possibly have been astray against Wasps that day, which was one reason for the major inquest after the defeat, Bath's first in the Courage League Championship since November 1993.

Peter Bills in *The Times* felt that it was wrong to play me at centre. He wrote: 'The chief miscalculation Bath made was to select their most astute tactician, Catt, as centre instead of at stand-off. The champions suffered grievously from Butland's inexperience in the role of pivot. Catt, who reads the game so well, would surely have inspired a more productive response to the position in which Bath found themselves in the second half . . .'

I don't know about that in particular! But I do know that it wasn't nice in the dressing-room afterwards. There was incredible disappointment — we took it so much to heart that Brian Ashton said he thought it would be a big motivational factor to ensure Bath went forward in a winning way for the rest of the season.

I make no particular excuses, but to a certain extent I think that some of the other teams in the league have finally learned ways to stop us playing. Another factor is often the heightened commitment of the opposition. For them, playing against Bath is probably their biggest game of the season, their own cup final, whereas for us it's just another game. That's how the constant grinding pressure becomes a factor.

Four league matches remained after that defeat, and we knew that we had to win all four to have a hope of regaining the championship, a trophy which must surely feel most at home at the Rec. It was all eyes then on what we considered the deciding fixture — against Leicester away on 15 April.

Bath should have had the league wrapped up before we walked on to the pitch against Leicester for what is always a difficult match. We shouldn't have drawn against Gloucester, we shouldn't have drawn against Orrell, we shouldn't have lost to Wasps. But somehow we did all of those things and it meant that we had to go into the Tiger's den to win the championship.

The match was billed as the Game of the Season, and right from the kick-off it began to drift just out of our reach, with Leicester putting points, and then more points, on the scoreboard. Once again the dressing-room was devastated afterwards; this time we knew that the Courage League was gone.

Bath did, eventually, fight back to within three points of drawing level in the second half in the gruelling contest at Welford Road, having been 15 points off the pace at one stage. But flying winger Rory Underwood scored a late opportunist try to finally crush our chance of a fifth consecutive championship, and a second consecutive double. It ended my dream of being involved in a league and cup double, an England Grand Slam and a World Cup win all in one season! The referee consistently penalised us for collapsing the scrum, when it was never to our advantage, and playing into a stiff wind in the first half we went in struggling at 18–6 down, despite taking an early 0–3 lead.

John Hall was furious with the ref. 'We don't collapse scrums . . . ever,' he said after the game, ' . . . especially when they could give away three points.' The guilty party, according to the referee, was that man Victor Ubogu again – the irrepressible Victor – and, not surprisingly, he was even more outraged at the decisions. Why should an experienced prop like Victor take the scrum down when we're 20 metres from our own posts? It would have been madness, it was not logical, but the referee obviously didn't see it like that. Talking to all the Leicester crowd afterwards, they were very sympathetic.

With those refereeing decisions going against us each time, it was not going to be our day. At half-time John Hall told us: 'Look, this is the league at stake, pull your fingers out and put a lot more effort in.' We did, but Leicester made the all-important first score after the interval, and only then did we begin to make our frantic comeback. It was always too late. First we scored with a Jon Callard penalty and then with half an hour to go I fed a long pass to Adedayo Adebayo who touched down in the corner, but Jon failed to convert, 21–14. Leicester added another three points from a penalty before we came right back into the frame after I scored a try, collecting an inside pass from Tony Swift, 24–21. But we couldn't pull it off, thanks to a combination of the ref, Liley's kicking, Jez Harris's drop-goals, and a real will to win among their forwards. The game was won by the Tigers, 31–21, when right at the death Rory Underwood collected that desperate last gasp overhead 'Dan Marino' pass from Gareth Adams and went over for the easy try.

They deserved to beat us on the day, despite the fact that the refereeing was unfathomable. From the moment the final whistle blew we knew the league was gone. We didn't think there was any way that Bristol could beat Leicester for us, and though the fixture against Sale was going to be the harder game for the Tigers, they beat them fairly convincingly.

Leicester, to give them their due, have done very well this season. Dean Richards has been a tower of strength, as always, and Jez Harris has done wonders for them with his kicking, particularly his drop-goals; they just kept flying over! All credit to Leicester, they have deserved their championship win.

I missed out on the end-of-season league clash with Sale at the Rec, the first time we had lost at home for four years, 13–18, and it was the worst way to finish the season.

Sale played well. They ran the ball, and they capitalised on our mistakes and scored from them. By half-time we knew the championship was 'officially' lost, with Leicester beating Bristol at a canter. It knocked any remaining heart out of the side.

It was yet another poor performance from Bath, with one eye on the Pilkington Cup and another on the World Cup. The greatest sadness, apart from losing like this at the Rec, was that our captain, John Hall, injured his shoulder in the first half and had to go off. It was his last home league match before retirement, and it was an injury which prevented him from playing at Twickenham in the Pilkington Cup final. It would not have been the way he would have wanted to go out of the game.

The championship had been lost long before this game, and losing our league crown made us even more determined to win the cup. We showed real character at Twickenham this year, and once again the team proved the sceptics wrong. We may have been pipped at the post for the Courage League, but we proved our mettle in the game's top knock-out trophy.

For what was supposed to be a poor Bath season, winning the cup and finishing second in the league was not bad! I think we've actually done damn well this season with the number of players we have used, and with the amount of disruptions we have had. Younger players have come through and have performed tremendously well in some cases, and because of that I think we've got a lot to look forward to next season. And mark my words, Bath will come back renewed again for next season.

This year many of our best players have been distracted by the World Cup. There are also other players in the Bath club striving to be selected for representative honours like England A games and England Under-21 tours, and the disruption has consequently filtered all the way down through the club.

We haven't been focussed or committed when we train. We have also lacked the discipline Jack Rowell taught us. However, we should still have been able to sort it out for ourselves; we're good enough players to have done so, but we didn't. The commitment should have been there for club, as well as country, but Jack has changed the ground rules. He's made us pour our hearts, minds and bodies into the England campaign, 100 per cent, and as a result we have had no choice but to hold back on our clubs. It was certainly not done behind their backs. England players were only allowed to play two league games for their clubs in April, for example. I think that was a sound idea because of the World Cup, but it was just one more disruption for Bath as a team in a terribly bitty and difficult club season.

Next season however, it is going to be completely different and we're going to be able to play throughout the whole season. There aren't any league games in the weeks before Five Nations matches, which is going to help us as well.

As far as I am concerned, I don't think our lack of focus on club matters has been Brian Ashton's fault. Obviously, running the team has been a new thing for him and we all feel he has done a good job under difficult circumstances – not made any easier by some power struggles backstage, something Bath RFC is unused to. Next season we're intending to restructure. We need a manager, in addition to a coach, somebody to really put their foot down and tell us where we're going, what we're doing, and how we are going to do it – and if you don't like it get out. That person will be John Hall, our new part-time honorary team manager, the unanimous choice of the players.

Off the rugby field this year I have been very lucky to have had a great understanding with my employer, Malcolm Pearce, and his company, Johnsons News Ltd of Bath. Rugby puts incredible demands on players these days, particularly once you start to break into the international game. As a top-class player, the time that you have to spend training, travelling and being absent from work because of matches and tours asks a great many questions about the game's continued adherence to amateur status. Without an understanding boss I don't know how players balance the demands of work and rugby against one another. People who want to pursue a proper career, like the law, have got to work normal hours, and in those circumstances it must be nigh on impossible to find the required amount of time for international rugby. And if they have families, it heaps on additional pressures.

With the amount of time I have had off, first for the 1994 South African tour, then an extra few weeks back home, and then the Barbados tour with the Bath rugby team, even before the World Cup, I would not have been surprised to find myself bottom of the popularity poll at work. But I wasn't. Malcolm and Johnsons have been very understanding and supportive and you need people like that in rugby in this day and age to help you get by. He deserves special thanks for everything he's done, for me and other Bath rugby players too.

After my experience working on the shop floor of the newsagents, I worked for Malcolm in sales and marketing at head office (when I was there!). Then in February 1995, with my rugby career progressing, we thought we could use my higher profile a little more effectively, and the company moved me across into the promotional side of the business working with Gill Wilson, my honorary second mother. She has kept me on the straight and narrow since I've been in Bath and is never scared to tell me where I'm going wrong. Thanks a lot Gill!

SIX

The Pilkington Cup: Winners Again

6 May 1995, and once again Bath are in the Pilkington Cup final at Twickenham.

Sadly, I missed the match. I had picked up a slight hamstring strain training on the Monday before the final, and withdrew early in the week rather than jeopardise my World Cup trip to South Africa. Our Bath skipper, John Hall, also missed the game because of injury, spoiling his retirement party. But Tony Swift, another Bath man bowing out after ten years' wonderful service to the club, played the game of his life in what proved to be a very emotional occasion and one of the best cup finals in recent years: Bath — 36, Wasps — 16.

Remarkably, it was Bath's ninth cup final victory in 12 seasons, and to cap it all, Tony Swift scored a memorable try to seal the match in the second half, giving the Wasps backs a lesson in sidestep and swerve on his way to the line.

His winning try came after Bath had soaked up heavy pressure, although things may have been different had Rob Andrew not had an off-day. Unusually for Rob, he missed two penalties, two conversions and a drop-goal. Perhaps his kicking had been knocked off course by the earlier announcement of Will Carling's sacking as England captain.

Two tries from often unsung hero Martin Haag, one from Ben Clarke, and another from Jon Callard, who also kicked four conversions and a penalty, ensured our victory and helped make the day a memorable send-off for Swifty and the injured skipper — who looked as though he collected the trophy with a tear in his eye.

We had a fairly easy run through to the final. In the fourth round in mid-December we beat London Scottish away from home, 31–16. Then, after Christmas, we won a testing fifth round away fixture at Orrell, 25–19, and I scored three drop-goals. The quarter-final game against Northampton at the end of February was at home, where we won more convincingly, 26–6. But the one game which really stands out, and immediately springs to my mind, was the semi-final against Harlequins at the Stoop – one of the all too few occasions during the season where Bath played some sweet rugby. It was easily my best game of the season, other than the internationals. Tony Swift scored two tries and we really enjoyed the game, something which has been unusual this season.

I think it was the third time that Bath have had to play Harlequins away in a semi. We were taken to the wire last year in a thriller when we won 26–25, having been 19–0 up after the first 20 minutes. Then I remember Harlequins came back to lead 25–19, until the majestic Tony Swift finished one off in the dying moments to take us through to the final.

This year it was a little easier and we scored a few good tries in winning 31–13, although I managed to damage my knee ligaments and had to go off yet again with an injury about ten minutes from the end. That's the second year running I've injured myself in the semi-final against Harlequins, as last year I managed to injure my ankle badly!

It was a good game, and one we desperately needed to win, and win well, both for the club and the players. Jon Callard scored five goals in a row, while Harlequin's full-back, Jim Staples, missed three early kicks which could have made the end result a lot closer than it was. I had a very satisfying day up against Quins' David Pears, making some telling breaks, and I fed Phil de Glanville for his try between the posts. I also had a good day kicking, with a cracking up-and-under which came down just in front of the Quins' line. We won the resulting ruck and again I made the pass, this time to the perfectly positioned Tony Swift to score the killer try. I then pitched in with a drop-goal before leaving the field limping.

The hamstring injury meant the build-up to the final was very frustrating. I genuinely felt I could not risk playing at Twickenham, for if I had, it would have been a monumental gamble. If the hamstring had given up on me in that final Bath game, there would have been no trip to South Africa, no World Cup. I spoke to Kevin Murphy, the England physio, and said that I didn't want to risk it. He understood, and so, too, did the players in the Bath team. They are all top-class players themselves and know the score. I had to take the view that the Pilkington Cup comes around annually and every year there is a chance that I can play in it (especially playing for Bath), whereas the World Cup only takes place once every four years. It's a long time to wait until the next one. Furthermore, I'm at the stage of my playing career where if I have a good World Cup I can make my mark on English rugby and make the England full-back position my own for a long time to come. Andy Robinson, nevertheless, took the mickey, relentlessly, but it was all in fun.

In addition to my absence for the cup final, we were also concerned about the absence of John Hall with an injured shoulder. John had gone off injured in the awful home defeat against Sale, the last league game of the season, and it meant that he retired on a bit of a sour note. He leaves a big gap in the team as a player and a great captain.

The atmosphere on cup final day at Twickenham was tremendous. It was a lovely day, and the swarms of fans looked more like a cricket crowd than a rugby crowd – shirts off, and sitting in the sun. As ever, there were a lot of people socialising in the west carpark, having their picnics, barbecues and a few drinks, of course. When the story of Will Carling's sacking was announced on the lunchtime news – his punishment for calling the RFU committee '57 old farts' – the carpark was suddenly buzzing. The Bath players didn't have too much time to reflect on the story, as they only found out close to kick-off time, but they were shocked. So was I. I really couldn't believe it.

All of the Bath players in the side had a will to win this game, more than anything for the two retiring 'old' boys, John Hall and Tony Swift. It was also a high-pressure game, after a hard season, for coach Brian Ashton, having taken over from the all-conquering

Jack Rowell. There was a lot at stake for Brian. If we had lost the press would have said the Bath bubble had burst, and perhaps pointed the finger at the new coach.

However, everybody was firing on all cylinders on the day, and focussed on victory. Phil de Glanville had a really good game and my replacement, Richard Butland, came in and did a fine job too. I hated being on the injury list, but the whole team played well, and it was just the sort of performance we needed to prove to the nation that Bath are still the best club in England, with strength in depth in their ranks.

For a man who was retiring after the match, the 35-year-old Tony Swift played like a fiend, and scored a fabulous try; a truly class try. I think he was one of the best, if not the best finisher, in club rugby right up to the end of his career. He was the tops when it came to finishing moves off and had the uncanny knack of always being in the right place at the right time.

I was also delighted that my Johnsons' work colleague and buddy, Martin Haag, scored two tries – his first points of the season – and what a day to score them. I was commentating on the radio with Ian Robertson at the time and when Martin burst through I accidentally lost control and started screaming down the microphone, 'Yeees, Haagie!!'. Ian had to tap me on the shoulder and say 'C'mon Mike, you can't do that on the radio. Cool down.'

It was a team decision to send John Hall out on to the pitch to lead out the players and to have him receive the trophy after our victory. Immediately the final whistle blew for full-time John said to skipper for the day, Phil de Glanville, that he should go up and collect the trophy, but Phil refused. John has done so much for the club and it was a nice gesture to make to mark his retirement, especially as we had turned on the style for him on the pitch.

John and Tony have helped bring on all the young players over the last decade or so, including myself. When I first came to the club I thought John was very arrogant and I didn't really know how to take him. But now I know why they call him Armadillo – because he is hard on the outside and soft on the inside! He never seemed to smile when I first knew him and always appeared to be a very serious person. But as I progressed through the ranks and started to play senior rugby, the ice broke. He began to respect me for what I was doing and he started to talk to me and help. All in all, John has been a big influence on my career.

I'm sure that John's mind never wanted to give up rugby and that's why the club has appointed him as the part-time honorary manager of the team for next season, working with Brian Ashton who will go back to a coaching role. John will be choosing the captain and vice-captain, and the management team. He will also be involved in the selection of the team with the captain. He'll be looking after us in the broadest possible sense.

John has so much respect from the players and the management that his appointment was given a unanimous vote by the team. We decided that we wanted him, not least because he has put so much into the club, and his loyalty cannot be questioned. We thought that instead of bringing somebody else in to the Bath set-up, it would be far better to get someone in who knows exactly how the club operates and who already has a good rapport with the players. With that kind of job spec. there is no better man for this new post than Armadillo!

John had a playing career in which *The Telegraph* correspondent John Mason says 'justice was never quite done' on the international stage, but for Bath he was one mighty competitor. It's unfortunate that he couldn't get to play in his last showpiece final, but if you look at what he has done for the team over this season, and the many others he has played in, we owe him a huge debt of gratitude.

I suspect that Tony Swift, on the other hand, probably just wants to stop, hang up his boots and concentrate on his work. In fact, by the time this book is published I'm sure that he will have already burned his boots! It was an unbelievable way to bow out of rugby scoring that superb try. I've never seen one as good as that at Twickenham, or at the Rec for that matter. He was very emotional afterwards. Tony has fully earned the remarkable record of having played in seven cup finals with Bath, and won them all. He will also be remembered as the highest try scorer in the history of the competition, an achievement that he can look back on with a great deal of pride. I hope I go out on a high like that!

SEVEN

Five Nations, Five Victories

I was on the bench for the England international against Romania on 12 November. Some of the squad players hoped that Jack Rowell would select the younger uncapped players to play in that game because we knew we could beat them fairly convincingly, but he stuck with the same opening side — with Paul Hull at full-back. It was the same story for the game against Canada on 10 December. But when I woke up on the Saturday morning before the match, I had the feeling that I was going to play. I even said to Les Cusworth that I really wanted to play; it must have been intuition.

Paul Hull received a nasty knock in the first ten minutes, and after 20 minutes he was off — and there I was, running on to the pitch at Twickenham again in front of a full house, and slotting into a team that was performing pretty well.

The match against Canada counted as my second full cap and I went on to replace Paul at full-back, which wasn't supposed to be my position! However, this time I was very relaxed, in contrast to my début international game — there wasn't a nerve jangling in my body. I was so relaxed and calm when I went on, even I was surprised. I remember catching my first high ball, which didn't pose a problem, and I kicked it smoothly into touch. It was good to get into the game with some tidy play.

For me, all the excitement happened in the second half when I scored my first try in international rugby. In one fleeting moment it changed my international playing career — and ultimately could possibly have changed my life. It was a very open game, and Rob Andrew — scorer of 30 points that day — was running everything, even in our own half. The ball went up and down the line. I'd been tackled, but scrambled back to my feet. Ben Clarke missed Rory out and passed to me on the outside. I went over and touched down in the corner. I was ecstatic and the crowd went crazy. It's not often that a replacement gets on, let alone scores, so I was very happy. I was also pleased with the way I was playing; coming into the line, the angles I was making, and the lines I was running.

I was involved in the other tries, too, either by going through gaps or picking people off, and I was enjoying it. I didn't have to do any defending either, and that was a bonus!

In the dying moments Rob took a pass from the scrum, fed it back inside to Ben, who broke through and, once again, I was on hand on the outside. All I had to do was complete a 30-metre run for my second try. I remember thinking, 'This is what I was born for – this is what I love.' I relished the space that day and the way things seemed to open up and happen at full-back. In truth, I have always thought that I can read the game a lot better from number 15 than I can from number 10 and that performance brought it home to me. The Canada international was easily my best performance of the season to date. I felt really comfortable wearing the shirt of the England full-back and I had time and space to play my natural running game. I also had the right mental attitude for it as well. But it was such a good experience that as soon as the final whistle had blown I immediately wanted more of that buzz and excitement from international rugby; I *really* wanted more!

After the game, which *The Guardian* described as 'one of the most ambitious counter-attacking games seen at Twickenham for years', a naturally disappointed Paul Hull spoke to me in the hotel. He congratulated me and joked that I was not to take his place in the team. What a cruel twist of fate for Paul and devilish good luck for me! But rugby is like that – one minute you are up, the next you are down – and the boot could be on the other foot one day. Perhaps that's what gives the sport its magic.

There were some other 'experts' there that night who thought that I would obviously get picked again because I had played so well, including one of my greatest fans, my mother, Anne, who was in the crowd. Stuart Barnes said that I had produced 'one of the most incisive attacking performances imaginable' – heady praise indeed. But I still thought it would be a bonus if I was selected for the next game; if I wasn't, I would be prepared and, indeed, happy to sit on the bench again.

When I came off the pitch after the 60–19 Canada victory, having scored two tries, I spoke to Jack Rowell: 'See, Jack,' I said, 'I've never let you down yet, and I'm not going to, so you don't have to worry about it.' He didn't say anything to me, other than well done and, perhaps surprisingly for Jack, he didn't say anything afterwards to wind me up or spur me on in the build-up to the next international, the Five Nations opener against Ireland.

Although I had played as a full-back throughout my school rugby days and for Eastern Province, since arriving in England I had only played at full-back in three games – once for Bath seconds, once for the England Under-21s in Australia, and then once in that 60 minutes for England against Canada! So at that stage you can understand why I wasn't really thinking that I ought to be playing at full-back for Bath, or that a positional change might help my game in the future. Indeed, I was quite happy to remain at fly-half for the club. If I got chosen for England at 15, it was a bonus. On one occasion I remember thinking, 'I may not be playing very well at fly-half for Bath, but at least I'm playing well at full-back for England!'. At the time I was, therefore, content for the situation to carry on indefinitely. If I had to play regularly at full-back for Bath and I played badly, Jack might reconsider my England position as a utility back, so in a strange way I was more than happy to keep on chopping and changing.

However, soon after the game, I started to think a little harder about matters positional. I've always felt relaxed at full-back, whereas at fly-half I've tended to be a bit bogged down and haven't always been able to get into my game. You don't have the time or the space at fly-half, and when I returned to play at 10 for Bath after the Canada international, I found that everything was very rushed again. I didn't really fancy it, and I sensed that I could now give more to the team at full-back. The more I thought about it after the Canada match, the more convinced I became that I wanted to play my rugby at full-back in the longer term.

Although I couldn't make any assumptions about my future England role, that's when I decided that if I got chosen for the Five Nations games next season, I would ideally like to play at the back for Bath. Jon Callard may feel differently though!

Coming down to earth after the Canada game was quite a difficult thing for me – returning from the high of top-class international rugby back to club level again is pretty hard for everyone, I think, not just me. But at least at Bath the nice thing is that there are 14 other internationals in the team who understand; they've been there, and they know exactly how you're feeling. The club's training session on the Monday night after every international is terribly difficult. They are the worst sessions of all because usually you're still thinking about the game on Saturday, and whether you're going to get chosen for the next international. You may be there physically, but mentally you're out to lunch. It was a learning experience for me on how to come down to earth again. You have to be very self-disciplined and tell yourself: 'Okay, I'm back at Bath now – this is where it all started, this is important now, these are my roots . . . concentrate.'

My performance against Canada immediately reaped rewards in that it earned me a place on the England squad trip to Lanzarote over the New Year, billed as 'warm weather winter training'. Incredibly there were 11 Bath players selected in the 33-man England party. The sunshine trip was a very welcome relief as I had a few pressing things to worry about over the Christmas break. The day before we left for Lanzarote, 28 December, I had to go in front of a three-man RFU panel to be quizzed about being 'paid to play' in South Africa – a terrific Christmas present! Thankfully, the RFU executive committee took no further action on the expenses payments I received while playing at home in South Africa.

That over, my best Christmas present came just a couple of weeks later. The team for the Ireland game at Lansdowne Road was chosen a week and a half before the match, and I was selected to start the match at full-back.

I was on the train coming home to Bath from London and John Taylor phoned me on my mobile to tell me the news. I knew the team was being announced, but I wasn't going to have a look at it because I was waiting, nervously, for somebody to tell me. I was so happy, but the problem was I couldn't show it on the inter-city. I couldn't really say anything or do anything, when I actually felt like getting up and screaming 'Yeeees!'. Although it was to be my third cap, it was the first time that I had been named in the starting line-up and that was a special thrill. I had my Walkman on and I can recall clenching my fists in delight. Five years ago I remember watching the Five Nations Championship at home in Port Elizabeth. Now I was going to play in it!

Back home in Bath, the first person I was able to tell was my South African girlfriend, Debbie. She was delighted for me. So, too, were my folks, who I phoned immediately. My older brother, Peter, immediately decided to come over to watch my first full cap. He flew over almost straight away for the Ireland game, and stayed throughout the Five Nations. My colleagues at work were also thrilled when they found out I had been selected. When I went into Johnsons, my boss, Malcolm Pearce, had already made a few telephone calls to round up the boys for a Champagne celebration and Steve Ojomoh and John Hall joined the party.

It all started sinking in. Some critics were saying I hadn't been tested at full-back, which was true, I suppose, and they also said that I was going to be bombed with up-and-unders at Lansdowne Road, where England hadn't won for some time. They were also arguing that I was out of position and would be a weak link in the England side, so a lot of needless pressure was put on me. But I did get a lot of reassurance from the team and from the captain in particular.

I've seen both sides of Will since I've known him. When Geoff Cooke was manager, Will was very relaxed, but not particularly liked by some players. A few of the older players in the team didn't really get on with him, or the Geoff Cooke regime in general.

Last season it was particularly strained as Will wasn't performing well. It brought the tension to a head. He was undoubtedly still a good captain and a good motivator, but it was increasingly difficult for him to call the shots and tell someone to pull their socks up when he needed to sort his own game out more than most.

Now there is a new management era and a new style. Early on, Jack Rowell must have had words with his captain and told him that while he may be the first-choice skipper, he still has to pull his weight to keep his place. It clearly worked.

Jack Rowell's management style keeps players on their toes all the time – you genuinely never know what he's going to do, or if you are going to play in the next game. I think that helped focus Will's mind, and since Jack Rowell moved the goalposts, Will has responded and proved a lot of his critics wrong. Now Will is playing some of his best rugby ever, and his contribution and enthusiasm is infectious. You don't want to let him down, or let any of the team down; now there is mutual respect where it was missing not so long ago.

The build-up to the Ireland game wasn't particularly tense, despite knowing that we had to win. We arrived in Dublin, where the weather was shocking, and caught a bus to the St Patrick Hotel. It was snowing, wet, and windy, and we trained in the bad weather on our arrival. I'm not used to the cold at the best of times, but it was bitter.

The Irish had chosen a new cap, Paul Burke, at fly-half, and I thought that was pretty good news for me because if Eric Elwood had been selected he would have definitely put some telling up-and-unders my way. Even so, I had been practising catching garryowens for some days in the lead-up to the game and, on reflection, I was grateful for the wind and rain in Bath on my final training night. Mind you, I dropped quite a few of those high balls in practice!

I woke up on the morning of the match and the weather was still changeable; when I say changeable, I mean it was making up its mind whether to snow or pour with rain.

It was the first time I had actually been into the England changing-room in a build-up to a game. It was deadly quiet. Nobody said a word and I soon discovered that was entirely normal for backstage behaviour before internationals. The players do not generally appear to get too wound up, and they don't bang their heads against walls or doors. There's no shouting and screaming. They try and focus, sitting quietly in their own little worlds. When you're on the bench you don't get to see all that. I had expected to see players like Brian Moore and Jason Leonard getting really hyper, but in reality it's just the opposite. They're outwardly calm, inwardly confident. Will Carling tends to chat to individuals as he walks around the dressing-room. Before this game, he was urging extra commitment, saying things like: 'Let's get in there, we know what we've got to do. We're playing into the wind first half . . . we've got to keep that ball tight . . . we've got to keep it in. We've got to be focussed. Know what you want to do as a player.' He talked to us slowly and calmly. There was no fever pitch of excitement, no fiery call to arms. It took me by surprise a bit.

The Ireland international was a game the England team were fired up to win, as the men in green have always been a bogey team for us, and it was a wonderful experience, despite the weather. The crowd were tremendous but I couldn't hear them very well as the wind was howling so badly. By the time the two teams ran on to the pitch the rain was horizontal and the wind was blowing even harder. There are two big stands at Lansdowne Road, one on each side of the pitch, and they created a wind tunnel that day; it was blowing a gale through there. I would kick the ball and the wind would blow it back over my head, it was so bad. We tried our best to warm up, but it was a complete joke. We were freezing.

Because the political situation was so sensitive at the time, the national anthem was not played, which was a great shame as it normally winds us up just before the kick-off – even me, a South African by birth! (The delicate politics also meant that the boys in the armed forces and the policemen among us – Tim Rodber,

Rory, Martin Bayfield and Deano – had to have personal security guards wherever they went.) Singing the anthem might also have helped us keep warm as well that afternoon because we were so cold by that stage. It was impossible to stand still because my legs were icing up. In fact, it was so unbelievably cold that one or two players were wearing wet suit tops underneath their jerseys!

The first 20 minutes of the game were fine and I was surprised that the Irish didn't continually try and test me out with high kicks because of the conditions. They only put one high ball up for me. I caught it, but Simon Geoghegan nailed me and the ball spilled backwards. We cleared up the loose ball and while I was on the ground I got my first rake mark from a forward who came running right over my back. I thought, 'aaaghhh, welcome to international rugby!'.

That was about it for me for the rest of the game. It was so windy that the ball was either going way over my head, or falling too short and going into touch. I didn't get much of a game really, and didn't touch the ball very much at all in the first half, mainly because our forwards played so well. We played a close game, kept the ball in, drove around the fringes and got Will running down the middle. It was when he was coming back to top form, and the way he played that afternoon proved to everyone that he can still do the business.

It was a very, very good 20–8 victory, especially as we were playing at Lansdowne Road where England hadn't won recently. I thought I had played a steady enough game, but I was conscious that I didn't do very much. Both my kicking out of hand and the few things that I did get involved in were okay, although much of the game was about trying to keep warm and pinching a quick chat with Jerry Guscott every few minutes. The main thing was that we had won, and won well. As a result, I felt that Jack Rowell would be unlikely to change a winning side.

The next hurdle was France at home at the beginning of February and I felt that this was a big one for me. I've always considered France to be one of the top teams in the world, and I would never have imagined in my wildest dreams that I would get the chance to play against the French in an England jersey, or even in a Springbok jersey – not this quickly! When the team was announced, there were no changes and I was naturally delighted. We met on the Wednesday before the match and had a fairly good training session. By then we knew our game strategy and what we had to do. We had already beaten France seven times in a row prior to this encounter and knew that their team didn't like coming to Twickenham. The French tend not to be very happy playing away from home, and I think that they must have dreaded playing England away in the Five Nations.

Once again the feeling was that I would be bombed with high balls, but it never transpired. The French put one up for me and that was it. England began the game just as we had against Ireland – our forwards were awesome. For the second match running, they built the platform for our victory.

I clearly remember the first ball I got at Twickenham against the French, a pass heading right for my feet. I picked it up and put a little grubber kick through and the crowd gave me a clap. That got me bouncing around a bit. It's an amazing feeling when you do something right and the crowd gets behind you.

Despite playing the French off the park, we were only 13–3 ahead when they scored a superb try. They are always so unpredictable, and that's why so many lovers of the game, me included, really enjoy the way they play and respect them so much. It's great entertainment. Some people argued that there was a forward pass in the move which led to the score, but the referee gave it – and whether it went forward or not, it was still a brilliant try.

The best thing that I remember about the France game was the try in the last minute, when Tony Underwood scored under the posts having broken down the blind-side. The move was worked out in training and called a Cat-trick. We'd only practised it three or four times and Brian Moore reckoned that it wasn't going to work. Jack Rowell, on the other hand, just said that we ought to try it and see – probably as it was one of Jack's moves! We were well up against France and the guys called the Cat-trick. I thought, here we go, now I can do my stuff. The timing was perfect, happily one of the strongest aspects of my game. I remember Tim Rodber in front of me and the French player coming on to him. When Tim fell to the side the Frenchman followed him down and the other player stayed out on the wing with Tony Underwood. Suddenly, a gap opened up for me and the ball was just sitting there, like it was on a tray. I took the pass and ran through the hole, but the defence was coming across and the full-back was also getting close. I wasn't going anywhere, so I turned. The only person I could see was Dean Richards, about 10 metres behind me, not the quickest of people. Then out of the corner of my eye I saw Tony coming through at serious speed and I just popped the ball up to him. He finished it off to end a really good move and the game ended in a comprehensive 31–10 victory.

After that try I thought my England place was secure for a while, at least, and the quality of the move itself made me even happier. The French were very aggressive throughout the game, as we had expected them to be, although, once again, I didn't have to do too much defensively, which was a bonus! I did a little attacking, but from my point of view the game was about being safe at the back and kicking balls into touch, both of which I'm fairly good at. I certainly didn't do anything special during the match, other than that break, and I was still hoping for a bit more to do in future matches. Nevertheless, we had a glowing press the following day.

Two weeks after the France game we travelled down to Cardiff Arms Park to play against Wales, another bogey ground for England. This was where the pressure was really put on me in the build-up. The experts were saying that Neil Jenkins had singled me out as a weakness at full-back and would focus on the kick and charge game. I was expecting it, and I tried to make it into a joke with all the press lads beforehand. I pointed out to them that there were going to be 14 other England players on the field with me, and I bet them all that Dean Richards would catch a high ball before I did. Behind the scenes Will Carling was very supportive, perhaps because he knew this could be a big test, and he took me aside and told me that he had every confidence in me, that I could do it, and that I was not to worry. The reassurance helped. Before the match I wiped any negative thoughts out of my mind and I tried to relax and convince myself that I could go out and enjoy it.

There was a brilliant atmosphere in the Arms Park for the game, played on Saturday, 18 February, the same day as Scotland edged out France in Paris 23–21. The stadium was buzzing when we took the field and when the Welsh sang their anthem it gave me goosebumps; the noise they generated was incredible. It's a very enclosed stadium and the feeling it gives you on the pitch is something else. I thought it was a brilliant occasion.

We were really hyped up for this game. We knew we could beat the Welsh and we did, comfortably, 23–9. Again, I had a fairly steady game. There was one high ball and Will took it, and that was it. I didn't get the onslaught I had been led to expect. I'm not sure why, but it may have been something to do with the build-up to the World Cup, with all the home teams keen to try and practise a more expansive game in advance of playing on the harder and faster grounds of South Africa.

Unfortunately, England sat back and started kicking again in the Wales game, and on a number of occasions when we could have run, and perhaps scored, Rob Andrew took the other option and kicked. There was definitely a feeling that we could have, and should have, thrown it about a bit more.

The one moment in the game that stood out for me personally was when I tackled Robert Jones, the Welsh scrum-half, after he broke through. It was just him, me, and the try line, and I caught him. It all happened so fast, as these things invariably do, that I didn't even have time to think about it. But when I watched the video afterwards I thought it was quite a good tackle! The other nice thing was that Rory Underwood scored two tries, and he had never scored at Cardiff Arms Park before.

It was so good to be part of a winning England side at the home of Welsh rugby and our convincing win set up a Grand Slam show-down against Scotland at Twickenham. With just three days to go before the game against the Scots Will Carling was more tense than I had ever seen him, there was a lot of bitching, and the atmosphere in the camp was horrible. We all knew what the problem was. A handful of the players in the current team had played in the 1991 Grand Slam decider up at Murrayfield, and England had been defeated because, according to Will, they had gone into the game assuming they were going to win. Will was now trying to ensure that there wasn't a similar attitude problem in the England camp for this match, but he ended up in a state himself. There was so much on the line for him. He wanted to win so badly and it created unprecedented tension in the England camp. In one training session shortly before the match itself, we were taking the mickey out of Will and I obviously went a bit too far — he nearly ripped my head off. Will made a bad pass to Tony Underwood, and as I was running back I said, joking, that it must have been Tony's fault that he didn't pick it up. Will tore into me and told me to concentrate on my own game. I was really quite shocked. I looked at Jerry Guscott, and he looked at me, and we shrugged our shoulders and carried on.

Running on to the field at Twickenham on 18 March was a superb feeling, and although the game wasn't a great spectacle, I did my job again. I remember making one particularly important tackle on Gavin Hastings and the ball spilling out of his hands. I thought I'd missed him initially, but I hadn't. If Scotland had scored at that moment it could have swung the game, so I felt good about the tackle, and my overall contribution to the famous victory.

Writing in *The Sunday Telegraph*, Paul Ackford commented:

If ever a tackle could justify the phrase 'try-saving' that was it. Catt has been England's find of the season. For years they have sought a player who offers a threat from full-back. Catt does. He is quick, elusive, but the best thing of all is that he provides tremendous angles for players to work off. He never hits the line in the same spot twice and he causes panic in defences every time he so much as sniffs the ball.

The Scots again indicated they were going to bomb me and this time Craig Chalmers did, quite a few times. But they were not generally very good kicks and the chases also weren't very effective. In addition, I had a lot of support at the back and, all in all, I handled the situation fairly well. It all made me want to get into the game more, and I made a couple of good runs in the first 20–30 minutes that really got me buzzing about the field.

The match was a real test and we were made to work hard for our Grand Slam win. The power of our pack, and Rob's golden boot – scorer of all 24 points, equalling a Five Nations points-scoring record for an individual – did the job. We put the Scots under so much pressure that they were forced to concede penalties and then it was down to Rob's trusty right foot, but we were never in complete control. The Scots really lost the game in the last 20 minutes, when Doddy Weir was caught in front of the posts after taking a dreadfully dangerous pass from Gavin Hastings. It resulted in Rob's sixth successful penalty and gave us a nine-point lead at 18–9. When Rob kicked a huge drop-goal to cancel out Gavin's penalty a few moments later, the match was effectively won.

There had been so much tension surrounding this fixture that there was more relief than pleasure in the dressing-room after we had won 24–12, signalling England's third Grand Slam in five years. It was an odd feeling. Rob Andrew said that the whole England camp was more tense than he'd seen it for a very long time. But there was something to laugh about, as well as the victory. Victor Ubogu must have been relieved to be able to take his own shorts off after the game – during it, he had not one, two, but three pairs ripped from him in what must be some sort of record!

Brian Moore moaned afterwards that the Scots had spoiled the game and that put a bit of a dampener on proceedings. He said in front of the television cameras: 'We tried to play good rugby, but we were constantly stopped by bodies coming over the ball the whole time. Scotland did what they came to do which, quite frankly, was not very much . . . Scotland ruined the whole game.'

Brian is his own person and he'll always say what he wants to say, and shoot straight from the hip. If we had lost, or referee Brian Stirling had missed any more of the punishable Scottish offences, I might have felt the same. However, Brian Moore obviously didn't look at it from the viewpoints of myself, Kyran Bracken or Tony Underwood – all of us playing in our first Grand Slam and soaking up the unbelievable experience. Not many people can say they've won a Grand Slam, and we didn't mind one bit how the Scots played!

Throughout the tournament Rob Andrew, Tim Rodber and all of the forwards were outstanding. Will Carling also had the distinction of being the first England captain to lead his country to three Grand Slam successes. But everybody made a contribution to the success of the team, even the replacements. I know what it's like sitting on the bench and it's not a lot of fun – going out and training with the lads all the time, but not being able to play is frustrating to say the least. The good thing about Les Cusworth and Jack Rowell is that they thank the boys on the bench and always include them in everything.

As a team we were happy with our victory and I think Jack was also very relieved. He must have been pleased to see us 'dog it out' against Scotland – evidence of our newly acquired resilience and self-belief. This season we have been up for a challenge, whereas last year the England team didn't seem to have that characteristic, and it was certainly absent when we played in the second Test against South Africa and caved in to defeat. Jack has toughened our approach since then.

It was disappointing that we couldn't receive the silverware at Twickenham because the building work at the ground was still going on. The English nation wanted to see their team with the Five Nations Trophy, and I wanted to hold it, feel it and do a lap of honour. But we did get to parade the Five Nations Trophy and the Calcutta Cup later on that night at the post-match dinner at London's Hilton Hotel.

I felt that I had performed well in the Five Nations games and I also felt increasingly secure at full-back, but it pays not to take anything for granted with Jack Rowell in charge. Paul Hull had a brilliant tour in South Africa last year and did nothing wrong against Romania. He was simply unlucky to get injured against Canada, which was not his own fault, and all of a sudden he was not even in the squad. With Jack, you're not guaranteed anything. I think that's good for the team, because it always keeps you on your toes. You're never really sure what he's going to do and you can't read him. I would like to think I've got a permanent place in the side, if not definitely on the bench, but who knows what's around the corner in rugby.

Jack Rowell has had a great deal to do with our international success in the 1994–95 season, and his home-grown psychology looks to have worked. Now he wants to win the World Cup — he *really* wants to win the World Cup. Jack has already won the Grand Slam, in addition to winning everything and more with Bath. During his years with the club he has become used to winning the Courage League, the Pilkington Cup, and the double. He is a hardened winner. The final challenge for him is a victory in the World Cup. He came into the England management team with that clear goal. Firstly, he had to reshape the team and kick-start it again while obtaining a guarantee of total commitment from all of the older players. Then he had to win the Five Nations Championship. All those initial tasks have now been completed and the squad has come together as a unit with a refreshing team spirit. Success has helped this season and so, too, has winning in style. Now we want to play together, train together, and be together; we want to win the World Cup.

I am going to relish the atmosphere as much as I can while it lasts, because it's only a short life in rugby. At least I can say it has been a brilliant season and that I have particularly enjoyed it, whatever comes next.

EIGHT

Jack Rowell – Confrontational, Inspirational

He's now got a lot of senior men playing incredibly well, and this is very much from his use of peer pressure.

WILL CARLING ON JACK ROWELL, THE TIMES, 16 JUNE 1995

If [Geoff] Cooke was the clerical strategist, [Jack] Rowell is the platoon commander: but always, as Carling observed, intriguingly, 'behind a tree' . . . Rowell has introduced subtleties which keep everyone on edge.

DAVID MILLER, THE TIMES, 16 JUNE 1995

I remember my first training session with the Bath squad and meeting Jack Rowell, a giant of a man, standing at 6ft 6in tall. We were not formally introduced so I didn't know who on earth he was at the time, but it soon became clear that this very tall guy with a loud voice, and a hot temper, was a key man in the club. It also became quickly apparent that he did not suffer fools gladly. He had a sharp tongue on the training field with a spicy turn of phrase!

I never had too much to do with Jack in my early days with Bath and I didn't really get to know him any better until I broke through into the first and second teams. It wasn't until Jon Webb's final game, when we lost to Gloucester 17–16, that we really crossed swords for the first time. It's the one early memory of Jack Rowell that really stands out for me personally.

We came off after losing and I had made this little chip kick in my own 22. I was sitting, dejected, in the changing-room with my head in my hands, distraught at having lost, and Jack whacked me across the back of my head. He shouted at me, 'If you ever play like that again, you'll never play football for us. You might play like that for Eastern Province in South Africa, but you're not going to play like that here in Bath.' Jack launched into me and before I knew it I had turned around and told him to fuck off. 'There's no need for you to hit me!' I said. Suddenly the dressing-room went silent because, as I later found out, players don't speak to Jack Rowell like that. Jack stood there dumbstruck, astonished that I had bitten back. He looked at me briefly and then stormed off.

Jack was clearly shocked and I think a lot of the other players were, too — me included. After I'd showered and changed he asked me to join him for a 'little chat' in the room next door. I had no idea what to expect. Once the door was closed and we were alone, he told me never, ever, to talk to him like that again in front of the players. He also asked me to go into the changing-room and apologise to him in front of the team. But I dug my heels in and told him that I wouldn't, and I repeated that there was no need for him to have hit me. I didn't see why I should apologise when he had been the one who struck out at me. That was the end of the conversation.

I didn't pass any comment to the team afterwards but asked for a word with wise old owl Gareth Chilcott, as I needed some good advice. I was worried by the stand I had made, and I'm the sort of person who gets really het-up over something like that. Cooch said that he was '99 per cent certain' Jack would apologise at training on Monday. 'He'll respect you for standing up to him for the rest of your rugby career,' he added. I wasn't convinced! It crossed my mind that I might never play Bath first-team rugby again and I had a fraught weekend worrying about what would happen at the next training session. Had I damaged my chances of getting to the top in rugby because I had got on the wrong side of Jack Rowell? I just didn't know.

Monday came after I'd been to a weekend England Under-21s training session, where I had been very downcast because of the argument. I was standing in the middle of the pitch and it was already halfway through the session. Jack was there but he hadn't said anything to me at all – and I hadn't said anything to him. Then he walked up, almost sheepishly, and much to my surprise he apologised. Jack told me that what he had done was uncalled for, but said that sometimes he gets so involved in rugby that he can't help himself; it means so much to him. To say that I was relieved is a massive understatement.

These days we get along without a problem and there have never been any grudges, but we don't do much talking – it's not that sort of relationship. In many ways I think our argument illustrates Jack's management style, because he uses confrontation between himself and players, and between players themselves, to get the best from his team. I also think that deep down he likes players to give as good as they get, although with Jack you can never be quite sure. You never really get to know him and his unpredictability keeps the teams he manages fired up and on their toes. Kyran Bracken once asked me if I had any idea why Jack had a downer on him. I said I had no inkling, but that he should just try and fight back as best he could. After Kyran started to do that, the situation began to resolve itself. Whether that was the reason things improved nobody will ever know. Jack continually tests his players and perhaps he was doing that to Kyran at the time. He works out what type of character you are and if he thinks that you're vulnerable, he'll rip into you to see if you can handle it; he'll always knock you down to build you up. It makes you go out and do even more to prove him wrong.

I understand that, when England played Romania last season, he played Dean Richards off against Ben Clarke for the number eight spot. Jack chose to tell Ben that he had won the position for the game only when he found the two players competing for the one place sitting next to each other! Apparently, he told Ben, 'Dean tells me that the place is yours for the Romania game only. He wants it back after that.' If that's not testing players and setting them off against each other, I don't know what is. But somehow it breeds competitiveness and has helped bring out the best in the team.

Jack Rowell is certainly an amazing and complex character — a self-made man who has the Midas touch, not just in rugby but also in the world of business. He was chief executive of food giant Dalgety before giving it all up for the joys of rugby union. He must have been a very shrewd businessman and pretty hard to get along with as an employer. But from a rugby viewpoint, there is no doubt in my mind that he is a genius. Jack has done so much with Bath over the past ten years, winning everything with the team including seven Pilkington Cups and four league titles. Bath have also won three doubles under him. It's a record that will probably never be equalled and part of the reason for that remarkable success is that he hates defeat, and instils that in his players. Without a doubt, Bath have missed him this season. He demanded and got total dedication and commitment to the club and, in his absence, that has wavered a little this year and consequently our form has dropped, although it is true to say that we've also missed certain star players, like Cooch, Stuart Barnes and Richard Hill — any team would.

Jack successfully brings all those skills he must have learned in business to the rugby field. At first he did it with Bath and now he is doing the same thing with England, and he has made those broad-based skills work for both teams. Before we went to South Africa Jack told the television cameras that he is a bit of a maverick — a man who likes to do things his own way. That's certainly true. But he does work with, and rely on, his team to translate those ideas into action. His wife, Sue, told the interviewer in the same programme that he was a 'good manipulator'. That's even more true! He's also very good at spotting players with talent. Jack brought Steve Ojomoh and Ben Clarke to Bath and I am more than grateful to him for introducing me to the England circle. He tends to recruit self-starters, ultra-competitive people, and then try to get the best from them by issuing challenges of various sorts. It works, and I often wonder whether he did the same in business at Dalgety. He is very good at being able to tell people that they are not the best thing since sliced bread and that they are capable of achieving so much more if they want to. But to get to that stage they have got to get a slagging-off beforehand! Typically, Jack's men are already self-disciplined, so we are also constantly challenging ourselves, as well as each other. There is a lot of peer pressure at work in a Jack Rowell rugby squad, as he encourages that. One way or another he demands, and gets, total dedication to the cause. It generally adds up to a winning combination.

Personally, he has taught me so many things, including how to handle people and how to express myself. He has also taught me how not to express myself and how to harness my aggression. But over the seasons I have played under Jack's management, the two most important things he has done have been to inspire me – he is the top man when it comes to inspiration – and to nurture my will to win, a will that has allowed all of his players a long lingering taste of victory, nectar to sportsmen like me.

I gave a broad smile when he became the England manager and coach because, having brought me up through the ranks, he knew about my ability. For a long time leading up to his appointment, Jack had been projecting me towards international rugby, both by recommending me to the selectors and by winding me up to give my best. In a way, I suppose, I felt that Jack's new role in the England set-up would help even more, particularly as I had performed so well for him at Bath. But I'm very glad I knew Jack and was already used to his individual approach before I was picked to play for England. For the England team players who weren't with Jack when he was at Bath, it must have been difficult adjusting to his style. I know for a fact that a lot of the players were a bit sceptical about him and weren't too sure if they were going to hold on to their places as a result of his appointment. However, I think that since Jack has taken over and injected his own thinking into the way the team operates, he has transformed a lot of the players. Rob Andrew is playing the best rugby of his career, and so, too, is Will Carling – and the best thing is that we are being successful, as well as enjoying our game.

Jack's first England tour to South Africa was an eventful affair. We won one test in Pretoria and lost the other in Cape Town, badly. Although we were not very happy with the way things went overall, it considerably helped to bring on a number of young players, including myself. It was a hard tour for Jack because he was under a lot of pressure, but the way he handled himself and the team was a tremendous credit to him. What else would you expect, I suppose, from a man who gave up a highly paid job at Dalgety just to coach the England side. He brought us through the Romania and Canada games undefeated, and through the Five Nations Championship with our heads held high, and before that he did brilliantly well with Bath in his last year. He likes being at the top, there's no doubt about that, and he will do anything to stay there. What Jack wants now, most of all, is the ultimate prize in our game, the World Cup, and I think he's determined to get it, either now or in the future. I wouldn't like to see his reaction if we perform badly and don't come back from South Africa with the William Webb Ellis Trophy this year!

And what of Jack Rowell long term? Jack ended his own rugby playing days because of a neck injury, having played for Hartlepool Rovers, Oxford University and Gosforth. The fact that his playing days were cut short may be one reason why he has put so much time and effort into rugby management. He certainly loves the game at Bath, and he loves Bath the club. I suppose in many ways it has been his family, so I would not be surprised to see him come back to Bath and work with the team again one day, in one rôle or another, if and when he retires from the England set-up. But let's hope he gets his hands on the World Cup long before that happens!

NINE

Will Power — Carling and Cash Hit the Headlines

On the Thursday before the Pilkington Cup final, England captain Will Carling appeared in a controversial Channel 4 documentary about the amateur status of the game, presented by well-known broadcasting personality Greg Dyke.

At the end of the programme, *Fair Game*, Will was asked to give his thoughts on how the game should be administered in the future. 'If the game is run properly as a professional game, you don't need 57 old farts running rugby,' he commented. Will's comments were given off camera and he thought that the microphones had been been switched off. As far as he was concerned the remarks were 'off-the-record'. The rest, as they say, is history!

When the *Fair Game* programme was screened it closed with Will's insensitive criticism of rugby's administrators and all hell broke loose. By Saturday lunchtime the story was out that our skipper had been stripped of the England captaincy and the betting odds on us bringing home the World Cup had been dashed. The news flashed around the carpark at Twickenham, where stunned Bath and Wasps supporters were warming up their barbecues for the traditional pre-match celebrations, the social curtain raiser to the club game's top match of the season. In many ways it spoilt what should have solely been a feast of the very best in club rugby.

I found out just before the team meeting for the Pilkington Cup final. Andy Robinson came up to me and asked if I had heard that Will had been sacked. I thought he was joking. Andy had actually read the news on Ceefax. Apparently, it was announced at 8.30 a.m. on the morning of the cup final — the biggest day of some of those players' careers. A lot of the World Cup squad were playing that day and it took their minds off the match. It must have affected Rob Andrew's game that afternoon — it certainly seemed to knock his place kicking off line. It also put an incredible dampener on the whole day, especially the post-match celebrations.

Shock summed up the mood of the crowd, who found it difficult to believe the extraordinary over-reaction of the men in authority. Later in the afternoon supporters from both teams jeered RFU officials as they walked on to the pitch with Prince Edward to meet the players, and some sections of the crowd began chanting 'Carling, Carling'. Clearly, the perception of the public was that Will had only been speaking the truth.

RFU president, retired solicitor Dennis Easby, aged 70, had made it quite clear that there was no way back for Will: 'It would be inappropriate for Carling . . . to represent England and, indeed, English sport,' read the press release confirming the sacking. Mr Easby also indicated that he would not, under any circumstances, reconsider the decision, which was taken without consultation with England boss Jack Rowell, who was 'specifically excluded' from the decision-making process.

The England players reacted swiftly, and, as I was injured for the cup final game, I was one of the first to go on the record. Speaking from the Twickenham touchline, I said that I thought the committee's decision was ridiculous and I was soon followed by other England squad members rallying to Will's defence.

'You can't have a chap who has served England so well for so long treated this way,' commented my Bath and England colleague Jon Callard. Jon also indicated to the press that the England squad would have something to add to the debate. 'We'll see the power of the England squad. At the end of the day, who is going to bring back the World Cup — the players or the committee?' he told *The Independent on Sunday*. A player revolt even seemed possible in the heat of the moment, fuelled by support from the public and, indeed, the press.

What galled the rugby supporter at large, I think, is that much of what Will had said in the *Fair Game* documentary was just comment at the time, despite the unfortunate reference to the '57 old farts'.

RFU secretary Dudley Wood argued in the programme that 'money is a corrosive influence', and that 'players need protection from commercial forces'. But Will, on the other hand, spoke for many of us when he said that everyone seems to do very well out of rugby 'except the players'. Rob Andrew agreed in the programme, airing the view that 'a lot of the committee do not understand what is going on in the world game'. While the southern hemisphere teams have blasted a huge hole in the rules on amateurism, the RFU at home has abided pretty much by the letter of the law. 'It's one rule for England, one rule for everyone else,' said Will.

Dudley Wood said he recognised the developments in the southern hemisphere, but argued that they do not have 'quite the tradition or the ethos of a sport played for fun that we have over here'. Rob Andrew countered, arguing that the game is 'more than fun now'.

He's right. It has gone far, far beyond a pleasant run-out with the lads on a Saturday afternoon and a drink at the bar afterwards. International rugby is a big money-spinner. It is now on a par with most professional sports and the game makes the same kinds of demands on its players.

Will should really have been more careful about what he said and how he said it – and perhaps he deserved to be ticked off. But the sacking was ridiculous. I thought there might be a disciplinary hearing or something after the World Cup, but with three weeks to go until our departure, I was amazed that they held a meeting and decided to strip Will of the captaincy. I would have thought it would have been in the committee's best interests, and the interests of the England team, to leave it until after the World Cup had taken place and then take whatever action they felt was necessary.

By Sunday morning Dennis Easby had a problem with the press and the public on his back and he was being pressured to consider a change of mind. Under the circumstances neither of the two most suitable candidates, Rob Andrew and Dean Richards, wanted the captain's job. Dean Richards, perhaps the player most likely to pick up the captain's armband bearing in mind Rob Andrew's participation in the Channel 4 programme, commented that he would not take the rôle, 'even if pressed'. He felt that Will's punishment had been 'totally over the top and outrageous'. As for Rob, I was surprised he was even considered bearing in mind that some of his comments were, in my opinion, worse than those made by Will!

The England squad players, as one, issued a carefully worded press statement through Parallel Media Group. We said:

> The full England World Cup squad respectfully request that the officers of the Rugby Football Union reconsider the decision to dismiss Will Carling. All the players stand fully behind Will as captain of the England team. We hope that this matter can be resolved speedily in order that we may concentrate on preparing for the World Cup without any further disruption.

Surprisingly, perhaps, Dennis Easby did not see the statement as a player revolt, describing it as 'very reasonable . . . a very conciliatory line'. It nevertheless turned up the pressure on him to rethink the dismissal, or find a clever solution to what was rapidly becoming an administrator's nightmare.

The players had already decided to discuss the matter among ourselves on the Monday evening. We had to meet anyway for training in Marlow.

The initial reaction of a few of the team indicated that there would be some sort of team backlash as a result of the sacking. However, I believe that the management would have dropped us all and taken another XV if we had said that we were not going to the World Cup unless Will was reinstated. I don't think they would have minded bringing in a whole new squad under those circumstances.

Other players in the team maintained afterwards that even if Will had been replaced off the field, he would still have been our captain on it. Brian Moore told *The Sun*: 'Once on the pitch, Will would have picked up the reins. He would have been skipper in everything but name.'

Thankfully, events overtook us. Mr Easby, due to retire in mid-July, was given an honourable way out of the media spotlight by Will's public apology, forged at a 40-minute meeting between the two at Twickenham on Bank Holiday Monday. Dennis Easby addressed the team in Marlow immediately afterwards. He arrived at training with Will even before we had a chance to chat among ourselves and told us it had all been sorted out. Then Jack Rowell got up and said, 'OK it's all over lads, now we've got to concentrate on the World Cup.'

The whole affair was laughable. By Tuesday morning the press was awash with our skipper's reinstatement. 'He gave me all the assurances I needed and I am delighted to be able to ask him to take on the captaincy for the World Cup,' said Dennis Easby. But, despite the U-turn made with some speed and prowess, the press showed no immediate signs of softening their stance on Mr Easby and his committee, and even now it continues to be ridiculed by the newspapers at every opportunity.

A significant number of committee members did not take offence to Will's remarks on television and there was also some disquiet in the ranks about the handling of the matter and the over-hasty reaction of a few people. The end result was that the committee was far more embarrassed than Will, so much so that there were immediately calls for Mr Easby to resign. The committee, nevertheless, closed ranks and gave him its full backing on the following Friday.

Personally, I don't think it's good to have people on the committee who have been away from the game too long. They don't have the first-hand experience of how the game is played these days and they don't necessarily understand where the game is going. You need younger faces in those positions, people who are going to be able to communicate with the players, take on-board their opinions, have a good relationship with them, and understand the complex commercial as well as sporting developments happening elsewhere in the rugby world.

After the affair, RFU president-elect, Bill Bishop, promised that there would be more money coming for the players. He also said, 'I think the players have felt we have let them down.' That sentiment was only too true. The biggest problem of all has been the lack of communication between the players and the committee, in fact, there hasn't been any! We have been trying to improve the situation for a while now, and that's why we formed a players' committee made up of Tim Rodber, Brian Moore and myself. But it has been fraught with difficulty.

I'm not sure whether it will be better with Bill Bishop and Tony Hallett (president-elect and secretary-elect respectively) at the helm of the RFU — I don't know what type of people they are. Dennis Easby said he was a players' person, but when he took up office it appeared he was just the opposite. The players who know the new men in authority say that they are sure that Bill Bishop and Tony Hallett will be much better. The trouble is that, at present, it's not just down to them, it's down to the committee of 57!

More than anything the Will Carling 'sacking' brought the simmering row over payments to players to a head in advance of meetings due to take place after the World Cup. Despite the reference to '57 old farts' making the newspaper headlines, much of the brief Carling fiasco, and the Channel 4 programme itself, was all about payments, and it was all just one more step forward in the difficult transition away from our strictly amateur game. Afterwards, Jack Rowell spoke for many when he said that the players don't necessarily want to be paid for playing. 'What they would like is the opportunity to earn off the field.' Jack added, 'What we have seen is a symptom of the tension as the amateur game of rugby changes.'

I, too, have got caught up in the simmering row over payments to players in the last year or so, thanks to my good ol' South African innocence, and I quickly found out that the issue of payments is a very touchy and newsworthy subject!

In October 1994 I received a call from a *Mail on Sunday*

freelance journalist called Mark Ryan. As it turned out, it was a call that could have brought my then brief career to a premature end. I had just been chosen to be one of the three England players to negotiate extra promotional money from advertising and sponsorships for the England squad, at meetings with an RFU working party. Mark Ryan called to ask me about my appointment.

During the conversation the reporter began firing all these questions at me. What would you like to see? Would you like to see players getting paid, and how much? Is it different in South Africa, and how does it work? That's where the line of questioning led me into trouble, almost entirely because of my honesty. I was new to all of this sort of questioning, new to the game here, and I didn't think anything of it. I kept on answering to the best of my knowledge and, in the course of the conversation, I indicated that I had been paid a 'match allowance' — a fixed sum intended to cover expenses — when I was playing for Eastern Province. Mark Ryan went on to ask me how many times I'd played for the senior Eastern Province side, and how much the senior players were being paid for expenses. He also asked whether expenses were paid at younger age levels and, if they were, how much. I answered all of his questions. I said that when you're 18, 19, or 20 years of age you receive about R50 per match for expenses. In my experience that edged up to around R150 when you played for the B side and up to R700 when you played for the senior Eastern Province side — the sterling equivalent when I was playing of around £150. He went on to ask me about signing-on fees, rugby league, and professionalism in the game in general.

I thought no more about the interview after I had put the telephone down. I believed that there was no harm in being honest and so I told him exactly how it worked in South Africa, where, as everyone knows, it is very different.

It was only afterwards that I became nervous of the consequences. I was driving down to Cornwall with my Bath team-mate Graham Dawe and I mentioned to him that Mark Ryan had spoken to me. Graham said that he knew of Mark Ryan and that other players felt very uneasy about his style of journalism. That's when I started worrying. But I still didn't realise the full ramifications of what I had said until the weekend when it was all published in *The Mail on Sunday* — and the outcry began. The splash headline in the newspaper was, 'Catt: I was Paid to Play', and afterwards the stories came thick and fast with headlines like, 'Throw Out Catt Now'. Suddenly, it looked as though I might face a life ban for being a 'professional'.

Whether the payments I received were legitimate or not, the fixed expenses given to me were easily justified by the travelling I was having to do in South Africa. Games aside, I was travelling to train with the Eastern Province squad four nights a week and, bearing in mind the distance I was living away from the training ground, those expenses were very welcome and used in just the way they were intended.

Even so, before too long I received a telephone call from RFU secretary Dudley Wood who said the committee would like to have a meeting with me to hear my side of the story. It was held at the East India Club in London and there were four of us present including Dennis Easby, the RFU president.

Thankfully, the RFU were very supportive. Dudley Wood indicated that he knew exactly what was happening all over the southern hemisphere, and I don't think the RFU committee was in any doubt about what was going on when I was playing in South Africa; they all knew that expenses payments were an accepted part of the game there. The RFU decided that no action need be taken because the alleged breach had taken place overseas and therefore outside their jurisdiction. That three-man RFU committee knew the score.

Perhaps I had been a little bit naïve in accepting expenses in South Africa. But as far as I was concerned, and to the best of my knowledge, I wasn't doing anything wrong. That's just the way it was at home and I had moved up the rugby ladder thinking that the expenses we received were entirely normal. It is worth remembering that South Africa was where my rugby career began and I imagined that the payment of expenses was the universal norm, both at home and abroad. I certainly hadn't thought to consider if it was any different in the other major rugby playing countries.

It was also reported that I had been 'paid' to play for Crusaders-Technikon. But that could never be regarded as a payment. We have sports bursaries to get into the universities and technikons in South Africa, which I believe are common throughout the world, and I had a sports bursary of R1,500 which helped me get into the Port Elizabeth Technikon.

I was happy that Will Carling sprang to my defence in the affair. He said: 'Every player we spoke to in South Africa during the summer tour made no bones about the fact that they were paid. Players here would explode if they tried to victimise Mike.' Some members of the International Rugby Board were also up in arms about the story for a while. My own view was that if the International Rugby Board had the power to require the RFU to ban me, then they would need to ban everyone in the southern hemisphere, and players from a few other countries a little bit closer to home as well!

I had tremendous support from some of the other players at the time – Jon Callard, Ben Clarke and Martin Johnson to name but a few. I also had support from journalists. A few members of the real rugby press rang and asked me why I had ever spoken to Mark Ryan. If I had told my story to them, perhaps they may have been a little more politic and circumspect, and not written an article which could have jeopardised my career. Thankfully, the whole affair eventually blew over.

The game is now changing quickly on and off the pitch. While the top international southern hemisphere players see the rewards for their sporting efforts, players in England still do not. Here, we continue to adhere to the letter of the law of amateurism, and while that continues to be the case, and we continue to play on an uneven field in comparison with players in other countries, there will always be tensions in the game between players and officials. It might not be like that for much longer. The chairman of the New Zealand Rugby Union committee on amateurism said in January 1995: 'Whatever people may feel about rugby going professional, we are already so far down the road that we have no choice but to advocate repealing the amateur regulations. The trend is irreversible. The present situation with its obvious "shamateurism" is completely lacking in credibility and does the game's image no good at all.'

I was listening to Aussie superstar David Campese recently and he said: 'The only reason I don't have a girlfriend or a wife is that they don't understand the commitment you need to give rugby.' It's true. However talented you are, you still have to work at your game extremely hard and the commitment is so great that relationships and careers must sometimes be sacrificed. Work in particular is difficult, sometimes impossible, given the demands of modern international rugby. The time for tours and training virtually rules out a conventional career, and without sensible recompense many dedicated players must struggle to make ends meet. That's why we should be looking at some form of payment in this country.

I told Chris Rea in an interview last year that rugby union has been my life for as long as I can remember, and that I would see no shame in making it my business. Why should I?

If press reports while we were in South Africa at the World Cup were anything to go by, the RFU was expected to finalise a deal to 'compensate' England players after the tournament, by virtue of a major sponsorship deal. 'Apparently' we rejected it while we were in South Africa — although both the supposed deal and the rejection came as news to me, somewhat of a surprise as I sit on the players' negotiating committee! Even now I don't know whether there was any foundation to the rumour, but the papers said the contract would have been worth around £6 million over four years, and that £2 million, possibly more, would have gone to the players for off-field promotional work. Divided among a squad of say 30, that could have meant just over £16,000 each per annum. The reports said that the sums involved were intended to be a supplement to our existing earnings, a compensation for 'lack of career-development we might suffer through rugby commitments'.

True or not, £16k 'compensation' would be neither one thing nor the other. In my opinion that sort of figure is not enough to compensate us for all but giving up our careers because of the pressure of modern top-flight rugby, nor is it enough for us to be able to give up our jobs and concentrate on the game.

Money-oriented discussions are now beginning to take place in domestic and international rugby circles, and they indicate that we are finally moving down the path away from complete amateurism, albeit at a tip-toe. But while we move at a tip-toe, the southern hemisphere countries are moving at a gallop. The thorny subject will come under full review when the International Rugby Board meets in Paris in August after the World Cup. I expect fundamental changes as a result of that meeting.

Professionalism, in some form, may be the answer. There's a lot of money being poured into rugby union and the players are getting nothing from it. I think that players should have the opportunity to earn off the field for taking part in promotions, advertising and personal appearances. I also think that England internationalists should be able to use the England jersey to their benefit. If you have done enough on the pitch to justify your inclusion in the England side, I don't see why you shouldn't be able to promote yourself as an England rugby player. I see no shame in that.

Right now, we've got to wait until August to see what the International Board comes out with. If they do not allow more 'flexibility', top-class players will almost certainly disappear to rugby league for the mountains of money they are being offered. If they are being offered as much as £250,000 a year to change codes, why not go and play? After all it's a short life when you're a top-flight sportsman, and you have to think about the future and providing for your family. One good thing is that IB chairman Vernon Pugh, also chairman of the Welsh Rugby Union, seems to understand that something has to give. He commented recently: 'We may have to recognise amateurism has been abandoned and then do our best to supervise consequent changes.' The time has come.

In the short term, I believe we should see players allowed to earn from activities off the field, even if we aren't paid for playing.

Longer term, I would like to see the management select an international squad for each season, or close-season tour, and pay them a set fee for playing, perhaps something in the region of £40,000–50,000. I don't think it's very hard for the RFU to commit that sort of money, they earn enough, and it is small beer compared with the earnings of most other full-time sportsmen and women. It would at least be enough money to allow England players to give up their jobs if they wanted to. I can see it going that way, but because our relationship with the RFU is not a good one at the moment, I think it's going to take a while before it happens, perhaps three to four years.

With more money on offer to leading players, rugby union could keep the rugby league scouts away. I was approached by a rugby league representative about six months ago. All he said was that I didn't have to make any decisions immediately, but that if I was interested I should give him a ring after the World Cup. I know that he's been speaking to a lot of other good players too, especially the New Zealanders, and he told me that quite a few are intending to change codes after the World Cup. There were reports in the paper just before we left for South Africa that Ben Clarke has been offered a £150,000 bonus if he promises to sign for Rupert Murdoch's Super League in Australia after South Africa, but I'm not convinced he would go, even if it's true. I am sure there will be others, however, who will succumb to the temptation, for temptation it is. I've read figures in the press as high as £300,000 for Ben, Jerry Guscott and Tim Rodber. Even I have been mentioned, depending on my performances in South Africa, although the man in charge of recruitment, ex-Aussie international Michael O'Connor, has been nowhere near me! It all puts the £22-a-day communication allowance we receive for playing in the World Cup in South Africa into perspective. It's not much when you consider that someone like Graham Dawe has to employ cover at work when he is away on tour; Graham is a farmer in Cornwall.

I wouldn't know the monetary value of my own ability at this early stage of my rugby career, but I'm sure that if the money was right in rugby union the players who are currently thinking about leaving the code would stay.

I love rugby union; it's my life. I haven't struggled financially so far, and until I've fulfilled all my goals in this code, I don't see why I should even consider changing allegiance to rugby league. I still have a few more ambitions in my union playing career to achieve, including playing for the British Lions and furthering my reputation, so that, one day, I will be remembered as one of the world's best players!

TEN

The Build-up to South Africa

England World Cup squad:

	CLUB	AGE	CAPS
Mike Catt	Bath	23	6
Jon Callard	Bath	29	3
Tony Underwood	Leicester	26	16
Will Carling	Harlequins	29	55
Jeremy Guscott	Bath	29	34
Rory Underwood	Leicester	31	75
Phil de Glanville	Bath	26	10
Damian Hopley	Wasps	24	0
Ian Hunter	Northampton	27	5
Rob Andrew	Wasps	32	65
Kyran Bracken	Bristol	23	8
Dewi Morris	Orrell	31	21
Jason Leonard	Harlequins	26	38
Graham Rowntree	Leicester	27	1
John Mallett	Bath	24	0
Victor Ubogu	Bath	33	15
Brian Moore	Harlequins	33	58
Graham Dawe	Bath	35	4
Martin Johnson	Leicester	25	12
Martin Bayfield	Northampton	28	22
Richard West	Gloucester	24	0
Tim Rodber	Northampton	25	14
Dean Richards	Leicester	31	42
Ben Clarke	Bath	26	17
Steve Ojomoh	Bath	24	6
Neil Back	Leicester	26	2

The inclusion of Leicester flanker Neil Back was the biggest talking-point when the 26-man squad was announced at the end of March, simply because of his size – only 5ft 10ins, compared with the towering 6ft-plus of most other international forwards. My Bath colleague, uncapped prop John Mallett, was also called into the squad, a tremendous personal achievement for him following a successful tour of South Africa last summer. But the delight at his inclusion, and of course mine, was clouded by the disappointment of the exclusion of my Bath skipper John Hall, who retired at the end of the 1995 season, and never played in a World Cup. In the past he missed out because of injuries, but this time he even missed out on selection.

Since the very successful Five Nations campaign, we've been training every Tuesday at Marlow Rugby Club and also some weekends. It's been very hard work, as it doesn't just end at the training; we have had to drive up to Marlow all the way from Bath, drive back the same night, and usually get up for 'normal' work the following morning. But good preparation is everything in this campaign, and we know that we will be at our peak in South Africa.

The build-up has been going pretty well from my point of view, although I was unlucky to pick up a hamstring injury near the end of the domestic season – the reason I had to miss out on the Pilkington Cup final. I won't begin full training until I get out to South Africa now.

One of the most interesting, and entertaining, developments according to the press is that we have been given acclimatisation suits to train in, which would look more at home on an astronaut. Will Carling initially tried the suits out early on in the year and decided that they would be a very good idea to help us get used to the heat and humidity we would encounter in South Africa. The suit itself is essentially a survival suit and I understand that the manufacturer does a lot of work with the Royal Navy. Our version is made without the normal waterproof coating they use, but it is essentially the same. The training suit is a bit restrictive and you feel quite cramped inside it. I found it very uncomfortable to wear at first as it makes you sweat so much and there's no air circulating; but I suppose that's the whole idea. It makes your body temperature rise and when that happens your concentration starts to wander. The thinking is that when we get out to Durban we'll be used to the conditions and more able to concentrate in the heat. I don't know whether it will work or not. I think it may be more of a psychological thing than anything else; having done four weeks in the suits, the players will at least think they are better prepared for the heat. You certainly have to consume a lot more liquid wearing these suits, or else you can feel very faint and tired after training. But as it forces you to drink more water, I would imagine that it also helps increase the overall healthiness of your body.

Training has gradually become more and more intense, and as we have come closer to our departure there's a lot more speed and power work, instead of endurance training, and it's all done wearing these special suits. Because of my hamstring problem I haven't been able to do any speed work, so I've been putting in a lot of effort on the weights strengthening my upper body.

On the training field Jack Rowell's coaching techniques, and the way he approaches and handles people, have not changed since he was at Bath; he knows what players can produce when pushed and he is a master at bringing out the best in them. Les Cusworth has also been a great success coaching the backs.

Away from training a few of us have had to compromise on certain key things. One of the big changes in my life, directly because of the build-up to the now imminent World Cup, is that I have been forced to reduce the amount of work that I do for Johnsons. I have had to move on to a three-day week at Johnsons and I think a number of other players have also done the same. I know that Tony Underwood has moved on to a half-day, half-pay arrangement, simply because of the amount of training that has to be done and the amount of time it takes. It's extremely demanding being a committed international rugby player these days, and people sometimes forget that. Amateurism has a price, and for England rugby players like me that means giving up your life outside work, and sometimes work itself. Dewi Morris felt he had to give up work altogether to concentrate on his World Cup build-up. But we wouldn't do it unless we loved the game.

The few weeks in South Africa may be the most significant of my life, and everybody else's life, so most of us have also virtually stopped drinking alcohol. I used to be a bit of a hooligan, out on the beers nearly every night, but now I'm a reformed character and I've stopped drinking for the cup campaign! Together with my Bath and England colleagues, we nevertheless went out on a liquid high after winning the Pilkington Cup. We had a fair few that night with John Hall and Tony Swift, but since then I've been very, very good, and I can almost say, with my hand on my heart, that I don't drink any more (ho, ho!). From a dietary point of view, however, we're still on what you would call 'ordinary food'.

All the players know what type of game plan we'd like to play under ideal circumstances in the World Cup in South Africa. We have been doing some tactical work on the blackboard, with Jack Rowell tending to take a back seat and let players lead the team meetings. Typically, he asks individual players, like Brian Moore for instance, to write down a few points on the blackboard, and then the rest of us will join in a wider discussion. It's down to the players, not Jack, to plan how we are going to play. As a close-knit team we communicate well with each other, and decide our approach at match-specific meetings like these. Jack will obviously suggest things. But, at the end of the day, it's always down to the players to make the final decisions, and to then go out and produce the goods; Jack doesn't expect the players to adhere to a game plan that they don't feel confident about. The plan for South Africa is to try and play a more expansive game, if we can, on the harder, faster grounds. I think that we proved we can do it against Canada and Romania last season, but, ultimately, our approach will depend on the opposition, and where we perceive their major weaknesses. First and foremost we're going to play a game that we think will win the World Cup.

I reckon that we have another 10 per cent left in the gas tank, and can play a good deal better than we did in the Five Nations

Championship. We have discussed a 'Plan A' and a 'Plan B' among ourselves. We can play the expansive, adventurous game, 'Plan A', and have the big runners like Ben Clarke, Tim Rodber and Victor Ubogu, hitting into the opposition backs, with the England backs peeling off, attacking the spaces and then finishing moves off – one particular area on which we have been concentrating in training recently, as we were disappointed that we didn't round off any of our moves too well in the Five Nations Championship. The alternative strategy, 'Plan B', is to use the kicking game.

My preference would be to play a more expansive game, because of my rôle at full-back, and we've got the skilled players to do it effectively. However, Rob Andrew is very experienced, and he knows what it's all about. When you're playing at altitude, as we will be in some of the games, the ball travels a lot further, and kicking may well be the best option. In those circumstances you're going to save your legs if you're not running around too much. In the end, it doesn't matter how we do it, as long as we win.

I have decided that the best thing for my own rugby is to try and move away from being thought of as the utility back, and concentrate on my rôle as full-back. In the past I've been happy to play anywhere, as long as I am in the team – Bath or England. But now I have finally decided that I want to try and win the rôle for Bath next season, as well as for England, and I would also like to take over the kicking duties from Jon Callard. I've been practising with a brilliant kicking coach, Dave Alred, for the last three months, and I'm back in the groove – just in case Rob Andrew gets injured in South Africa and Jack Rowell turns to me. I suspect he may go for Jon in that situation, but I feel I'm ready to do the job if asked. With Dave's help, I think I've got it in me to be England's next place kicker, sooner or later. It's Dave, after all, who has helped Rob Andrew so much.

We've been sent the videos of games between Argentina *v* South Africa, Italy *v* South Africa, Argentina *v* Ireland, and Western Samoa *v* South Africa, and all of the players in the team have watched them. We haven't sat down and watched them together, as a team, as they were sent to us at home. But when we have come together in training, we have talked about each of the games, discussed how we should play against the different teams, and talked in detail about the strengths and weaknesses of our pool group opposition.

As far as the England team are concerned, I think that the performances of Rob Andrew, Ben Clarke and Tim Rodber are going to be the keys to our success in South Africa, although everybody will have to play up to their potential. Will Carling and Jerry Guscott are going to be important figures, but ultimately I think the team's performance will hinge on Rob's goalkicking and the dominance around the scrum that can be provided by Ben and Tim. They all need to produce the goods for the team to play well.

Jack called us together one Monday evening recently and told us that not everybody in the squad would play in the World Cup, so it's obviously in his mind that he's going to play the best team in every game if he can. It certainly fired us up for training!

We know we're in one of the hardest pools and will have a very difficult run-in to the final. England have got to play nearly all of the best teams in the tournament to go all the way. Whatever happens we don't have an easy run through. We should, on paper, beat every side, so let's hope that we can get through the pool fixtures injury-free and concentrate on beating South Africa or Australia in the quarter-final, before we think about the semi-final or the big one — the final. Virtually all of the other teams in the tournament pose a threat of some kind, and much of our success will depend on how we play on the day. We know we can beat New Zealand, we know we can beat France and Scotland. In fact, if we play well, we know that we can beat all of the teams in the cup.

I think that South Africa and Australia are going to be the most formidable opposition. My dad has told me that there's Rugby World Cup fever brewing in South Africa, but the Springbok side are under a lot of pressure to produce the goods as they are the home nation. The South Africans have got good enough players to go all the way, but they are inexperienced, and the team that has been chosen hasn't really been able to play together very much, which could be a disadvantage for them. They have continually chopped and changed their side, as well as their management, which must have been very disruptive. And that opening game, Australia v South Africa, is sure to take plenty out of both of the teams, physically and mentally. Both of them will want to win that match very badly, if only to avoid England later on!

I would love to play against my home country, and beat them. I'd also love to play against them because I know some of the South African players of old, guys like André Joubert (a player who would certainly make my World Cup Fantasy League team) and Hennie Le Roux – who used to be a team-mate of mine. I think it would give me the ultimate satisfaction and, to be honest, I think we would rather play South Africa in the quarter-final if we get there. Australia are an unknown quantity at the moment, and dangerous when rattled. The Wallabies are still not firing on all cylinders, although being world champions you have to assume that they will be well prepared for this competition by the time they arrive. Of the other teams which pose a special threat, New Zealand are always very hard, and France can be brilliant one moment and terrible the next.

There is a great team spirit among the England squad, and with everything that has happened over the past few weeks, not least the Will Carling fiasco, I feel it may even have helped unite the team even more. We have been meeting so frequently that we've got to know each other's style of play, and now it is all falling into place. However, ideally, I would have preferred the England team to have played one more warm-up game before going to South Africa, even if it was against Bath, Leicester or one of the divisional sides.

When we get out there, getting our mental approach right will probably be the last remaining, and possibly the biggest, hurdle for us to clear. We are fitter, bigger, faster and heavier than ever before, but everything has to be right in our minds for us to win the tournament. Success in sport today can be as much about the mental preparation and attitude, as talent, and that is why we are taking a sports psychologist with us on the trip. Different players have different ways to relax; they either go to watch movies, take a stroll around town, or go and get their hair cut. Some of them, like Steve Ojomoh, enjoy playing video and computer games. I expect that I will be on the phone talking to my mates, or sitting on the beach. I might watch a bit of television and hopefully the hotels will have games rooms so that we can play snooker. Cards are also popular. I reckon that the players' card school is going to be huge this time around – possibly the biggest ever. Myself, Dean Richards, Ben Clarke, Will Carling, Kyran Bracken, Dewi Morris, Phil de Glanville, and Jon Callard should all be playing. It's probably the main reason why we want to be paid, because, one way or another, we invariably end up losing all our money! Backgammon is another favourite leisure pastime on tour, and I'm sure it will be popular in South Africa. I know for a fact that John Mallett and Phil de Glanville are planning a big competition, because Phil beat John in Barbados last year on the Bath tour, and John wants his money back. Golf will be equally high on the list of priorities. There are lovely courses throughout South Africa and playing out in the sunshine will be very relaxing. For the most part, I'll probably meet friends and family, and I'm looking forward to my folks coming up to Durban when I'm there.

Our wives and girlfriends are invited out to South Africa for a while, too, but, according to the schedule, we only really see them twice in the three weeks we're out there. My girlfriend, Debbie, will make the trip. She's South African, so it's a marvellous opportunity for a free trip home for her. The girls will watch the three pool games, at least, and possibly the quarter-final. We have one or two barbecues pencilled in on Sundays and we'll probably see them there as well. It's a long time to be without the girls – five weeks – especially for players with families, but at least on the tour we will have some contact.

All of the teams who are in the quarter-finals and semi-finals move up to stay in Pretoria and Johannesburg for the closing stages so, if we get through the pool games, we'll be living around there for the rest of the tournament and we will fly down to Cape Town the day before the game, or games, if we end up playing there. So, I hope to spend some time around the Jo'burg area, where Debbie's parents live.

As we move ever closer to our departure for South Africa, the press have been giving extended coverage to the team and its plans. Together with the training, the many end-of-season dinners, awards ceremonies, appearances and events, it's a really hectic schedule – a media circus. So much so that I am becoming forgetful! On my way into London last week, I realised that I had forgotten my dinner jacket for the RFU Awards Dinner in town that night and I had a real panic trying to get a suit sorted out. I only managed to find a DJ that would fit me at 7 p.m., half an hour before the dinner, and it was just as well as I was nominated as one of the RFU's Players of the Season, together with Rob Andrew and Martin Bayfield, who won the award. I have also received the Whitbread Flowers Most Promising Player of the Year Award. I feel it's a great honour to be so well thought of, and it makes me very proud.

Perhaps the most amusing function has been the packed National Sporting Club Dinner at the Café Royal. Our manager, Jack Rowell, was hilarious, and picked out Victor for some special barracking. He said that the team was worried when Victor arrived at training one day with love bites on his neck, but that we were not to be concerned because they were all self-inflicted! The dinner was great fun, and a terrific send-off. There were 600 people there, and Jack spoke for 45 minutes – although I have to say only the first 20 were entertaining!

I don't go back to South Africa with mixed feelings. I was an outsider when I broke into the Eastern Province team when I was at home, and felt very much like a foreigner in the dressing-room. They all spoke Afrikaans and, although I could understand the language, I was not confident enough, or good enough, to speak back to them in their own tongue; and they certainly wouldn't speak to me in English. It was quite a hostile atmosphere and it was also intimidating. But it hasn't been like that playing in

England with Bath, or for the national team. I have always felt much more at home, and more comfortable, in the dressing-room, and it has helped my game.

Nowadays, I'm an England player through and through and, as far as I am concerned, it's them and us. I know that if we play South Africa in the quarter-finals or semi-finals, we can beat them, and I can't wait.

It's also important for me to do well in this World Cup, after all, it could change my life if I have a good tournament.

ELEVEN

The Tension Mounts in Durban

This season's main event is upon us, the tournament all the England players have been working towards for so long. For many players, it is the pinnacle of their careers. For me, it's even more than that, it's a dream come true; playing for England in the World Cup 'at home' in South Africa.

LONDON TO JOHANNESBURG – WEDNESDAY, 17 MAY

We met up at the Petersham Hotel yesterday; the squad are now in a state of high excitement.

It was tiresome waiting to leave today, when we were so keen to get away, but I can safely say that we are more than happy to be leaving the English weather, as it's literally pouring with rain. I'm probably more excited than anyone else in the squad as I'm going home again, and will get a rare chance to see those closest to me as well as playing in the rugby tournament of my life.

We left London Heathrow at 6.30 p.m. and having waited for so long, there was a definite buzz of excitement as we boarded the plane. The angst had begun!

The flight to Johannesburg was extremely quiet and restful. We were lucky enough to travel Business Class as guests of one of the key World Cup sponsors, South African Airways; apart, that is, from the biggest and tallest in the squad – the six foot tenners – who were upgraded to First Class. Being neither big nor tall, I was not so lucky, and those upgraded got plenty of flack (and visits) from the boys in Business – especially from team members who are keen on their computer games. Those games in First Class are really something else! The Irish team were also with us on the other side of the plane.

It was a very good and enjoyable flight thanks to SAA. Everybody had the chance to grab some sleep and relax, and there was no hassle at all which gave us the chance to think about what the next five weeks might have in store – everybody, apart from Victor who was walking up and down the plane with his camcorder and videoing the luxury experience for future screening at his new bar in Chelsea, Shoeless Joe's! He got quite a ribbing for that and was told in no uncertain terms that if he wanted to shoot revealing footage of the squad at rest, he should do it along with the proper television crews, at the allotted times!

There is a very different atmosphere to that when we left on the tour last year – this trip is not a jolly, this time it is for real, serious hard work. We're going out to be committed workmen.

Here we go, the quest for the World Cup, the William Webb Ellis Trophy – or 'Bill' as it is affectionately known in Australia since they won it!

ARRIVING – THURSDAY, 18 MAY

We arrived at Jan Smuts in Johannesburg at about 7.30 a.m. Sadly, it was all a bit of a let-down as there were no press, media or public around to meet us. The officials decided to divert both teams away from the public area to stop any fuss being made, when on this occasion it would have been welcome! It was very different from last year when we got a rousing reception on the way in. This time there was just silence and wide empty halls, and it was a bit of a disappointment – especially as we were arriving for the World Cup. We waited for three hours to catch the plane to Durban and hardly saw a soul, although we felt a little chirpier when we arrived in our pool group destination to find that the sun was shining and it was a beautiful day.

We had a fairly low-key arrival in Durban, too, around lunchtime. We were taken from the plane straight to the hotel, again diverted away from the gaze of the public. I think much of this is down to the security aspect, and understandably so, for such a big, high-profile event; for that reason, I suppose, we can't complain too much.

We're staying at the Holiday Inn in Durban, a budget-style beachfront hotel, but not the one the England management had initially earmarked for us. We had wanted to stay in another hotel, a little out of town, where there is some peace and quiet. However, the organisers of the competition decreed that all teams must stay in the same sort of accommodation, so the Holiday Inn it is, right in the thick of the action in Durban, a busy holiday resort.

At least the hotel management has been able to find six longer beds for the taller guys in the team! I was given a room on the seventeenth floor, sharing with Kyran Bracken, the bookworm. There were plenty of messages for me from friends and family; I'm back home and it feels good with the sun shining and a view of the sea.

Joe Kool's, the city's top disco and bar is close by, and apparently it never closes, but I don't think we'll be visiting it too often, not late at night anyway. We're pretty much off the drink and, to date, everyone is being very sensible and dedicated – dare I say professional! It's early days though.

Apparently, the team has a very different and more determined attitude to the one which played in the last World Cup. Four years ago England were effective but predictable. Now we are generally fitter, stronger, taller and better prepared, mentally as well as physically. We are also more mobile and flexible, particularly among the forwards. Let's hope it makes the difference. I would imagine all the other top teams in the tournament fear us more than we fear them.

We have been told that there will be a big drive on drug testing in South Africa and random tests will be carried out throughout the whole tournament. Any player who gets caught will be on the first plane home. Two of our squad were asked to provide samples as part of the random testing today. Frequent tests are going to be made, two players on each team every time we play.

After a bit of a run to loosen up, the team held a press conference where I met some of the South African journalists I know from when I lived here. Later on, we relaxed a bit and played Frisbee on the beach, which was quiet as it's Thursday afternoon.

After a few hours' rest, under orders, our first intensive training session took place in the ground where we will be playing our pool games, King's Park. It was still hot, right up in the 80s. But I think the acclimatisation suits we've been training with in England helped. When I think back to last year's tour of South Africa, which helped prepare us mentally and physically for this campaign, I remember the struggle we had getting used to the conditions. Here, I already feel that it has been easier to get into things.

It's humid where we are in Durban, whereas in Cape Town the conditions are almost English, and the altitude is the big factor in Jo'burg. I think we all feel the teams which will do best in the cup are those which can adjust to the different climates and conditions. After last year's experience, the England boys really believe we can play anywhere. Jack also convinced us to widen our attacking horizons on that tour, which stands us in good stead for the more open game we hope we can play over here.

We trained at 5 p.m. for a couple of hours. My hamstring felt pretty good after an initial stretching session and afterwards we had a bit of a knock-around. It was only meant to be a 50 per cent commitment contact game, but it didn't feel like it. A lot of the players had energy to burn, probably because of the long journey, and also because we had not trained for three days.

We had a team meeting afterwards. Will stood up and asked us if we were prepared to attend lunches while we're here, sign balls etc. We agreed to sign the balls but decided that we would not attend lunches or make any personal appearances, which we felt could distract us. Jack told us exactly what he wanted from us, and he put it straight on the line. It's the first time I've ever heard him swear in a team meeting, and it put us on our guard. The atmosphere has already started to become a little more tense.

Nobody is allowed to go out on the beers, but Jason Leonard, Kyran and I went down to Joe Kool's on the beachfront to get out of the hotel, and I had one superb South African Castle lager — it's great to taste that again.

I spoke to my dad this morning and it was a nice change not to have to worry about how much the phone call was costing. Then I spoke to my younger brother, and my cousin, who told me that she is two months pregnant. Mum is very excited that I'm here.

FRIDAY, 19 MAY

Tour Judge Damian Hopley elects his court for the tour, but who knows when we will get a chance to have a serious court session! Dean Richards and Martin Bayfield are the enforcers, Brian Moore will prosecute, and my roomy, Kyran Bracken, will have the virtually hopeless task of defending anyone who is accused. Damian also has to choose the Dick of the Day, awarded to any of the party, including the management, who does something foolish or untoward.

A lot of the squad have nicknames. Victor is already being called 'Clueless Joe', after his new sports bar, Shoeless Joe's. The bar itself also has a newly acquired nickname, 'Beerless Vic's', as it proved a bit difficult to get a drink when we went down there for the opening! Quite a few of the other nicknames are based on my esteemed colleagues' physical features. Will Carling is called 'Bum Face', for instance, because of his cleft chin. I also like Kyran Bracken's — 'Village' — because he is a bit scatter-brained. John Mallett is called 'Barry White' because of his voice, and Dewi Morris is 'The Monkey'. Brian Moore also has a good nickname, 'Tojo', after a Japanese general. (Ojo later picked up the unfortunate tag 'Ugly' after being nominated as one of Gareth Chilcott's 'most unattractive players of the tournament' on the television.) At least the boys haven't picked up my schoolboy nickname, 'Fox', which I really used to hate.

I woke up very tired from the jetlag, and stiff after yesterday's initial session; my first for sometime. It's another sunny day in paradise. After lunch, a stroll, a swim and a snooze I tried out Kyran's new kicking, throwing and passing net.

We had a hard training session in the afternoon, and my legs felt a bit tired, but I'm feeling pretty good – and confident. Rob and I had a kicking session after training.

I spoke to a few old friends and then went down to Joe Kool's where I saw a few more mates. But we only had two beers; we've been very good so far. On our way back we heard a load of sirens going. Apparently, three men had mugged a tourist outside the hotel. As we were listening to our security guards' walkie-talkies to hear more news, there was another incident which flashed over the airwaves where someone had pickpocketed a lady tourist in a phone box! It's disappointing to see crime like this in Durban, and beggars and small children asking for money on the street, and there really are a lot of thefts going on.

It's 10.45 p.m. now and I'm sitting on the lovely long beach listening to the waves rolling in, with the moon shining on the water . . .

SATURDAY, 20 MAY

It's the most exciting day of the tour so far – I'm being sarcastic, of course. We were up at 7.15 a.m. to catch a plane to Cape Town for the opening luncheon, the official opening of the World Cup – the brainchild of the organisers. Everybody was tired, and not in the mood to go.

The teams from Tonga, Western Samoa, Japan and Wales were on the same plane as the England lads, all in our 'number ones' sweating away. It might have been a lovely day in Durban, but it was horrid in Cape Town, pouring with rain, and it was a bumpy two-and-a-half-hour flight to Cape Town as a result. Steve Ojomoh wasn't looking too good on the flight!

When we arrived we piled into the coaches provided for a 30-minute ride down to a winery in Stellenbosch. Nobody was talking, nobody was excited. We arrived at a white marquee in the middle of nowhere with the wind howling and the rain peeing down – there was less than no enthusiasm whatsoever from any of the teams, and our worst fears were confirmed.

All the players from the 16 teams flew in and all of us were kitted out in our smart colourful team blazers, but in most respects it was a waste of a day. Despite receiving a cap and a little trophy for playing a part in the World Cup, there was a very flat atmosphere. I was talking to Rob Andrew, who had been to the 1991 opening luncheon, and he said it was the worst one he had been to, and I believe him! The luncheon really was as boring as hell; very dull and very dry. We all felt that having recently arrived, it was the wrong time on the tour to do that to us.

The Welsh were already on our plane when we boarded, and had to get up at 5.30 a.m. in Bloemfontein to get the flight. It was ridiculous. Why couldn't it all have been done by satellite television? The official Scottish team 'uniform' provided the entertainment highlight for the England team, although we did have a chuckle when the organisers left New Zealand out of the presentations by accident.

From what I have seen and heard today, the South Africans have a lot of pressure on them; I don't know how they sleep. They, nevertheless, seem very confident. We also had a chat to the Welsh team, and some of the other players we know. I saw David Campese talking to Jerry, and Will and Rob chatting to Tim Horan. It's good to talk! We might not have the chance, or the inclination, later on in the tournament.

We got on the flight back to Durban at about 4 p.m., and lifted off around 5 p.m. The first seven in the alphabet got into First Class which made it a better journey for me considering the bad weather – the plane was all over the place again. When we arrived back at 7.30 p.m. there was another half an hour on the bus, and by this time the boys were really hacked off!

I went out for a run when we got back, and then down to Joe Kool's for a quick beer. Today has been a disappointing day considering it is the beginning of the World Cup, one of the biggest events of my life. In fact, it was all a load of rubbish!

SUNDAY, 21 MAY

It's the hottest day so far and it made training harder, particularly with all the boys climbing in, and the tension building up.

Afterwards we went to a private beach about ten minutes away and had a pleasant lunchtime barbecue.

MONDAY, 22 MAY

Today the team to play against Argentina is being named, so this morning's training session is ultra-competitive and intense, with some squad players making a desperate effort to impress Jack.

When the team is announced, Dewi Morris is a surprise recall, and he will start against Argentina. Dewi retires after this tournament. He took six months unpaid leave from his job in the run-up to the World Cup so that he could dedicate all his time and effort to rugby — so all power to Dewi, he deserves a break. He was understudy to Richard Hill in the 1991 World Cup, but was one of the two players in the 26-man squad who did not get a game. It's a bit of a dream come true as a result, but it's tough on my roomy, Kyran Bracken, who did so well in the Grand Slam games. Kyran's out, and perhaps it has something to do with his attitude. Sadly, he hasn't impressed some of the people with his approach to things out here. Kyran spends plenty of time on the beach and, as well as reading all the time, he sleeps a lot. Ojo is also in for Dean Richards.

Doc Terry Crystal is awarded Dick of the Day by Damian for getting caught out at the beach barbecue on Sunday. He was spotted pouring beer into an empty Coke tin so he wouldn't get caught drinking, and then had the nerve to castigate Jack for setting a bad example for downing a bottle of lager! As a result the Doc had to wear a ridiculous cowboy shirt for the rest of the day.

The team had another hard session this morning, and then I did some kicking. We desperately need a game to get into things.

Later in the day I played golf with Jerry at the superb Durban

Trying to get a unique move sorted out during one of the Cellnet Rugby Roadshow sessions prior to the 1995 World Cup (David Rogers, Allsport)

I played at fly-half against Western Samoa in the 1995 World Cup and relished the opportunity to get the team running. Here I am, leading the charge
(David Rogers, Allsport)

Flexing my muscles during the World Cup trip — not a New Zealander in sight, thank goodness! (David Rogers, Allsport)

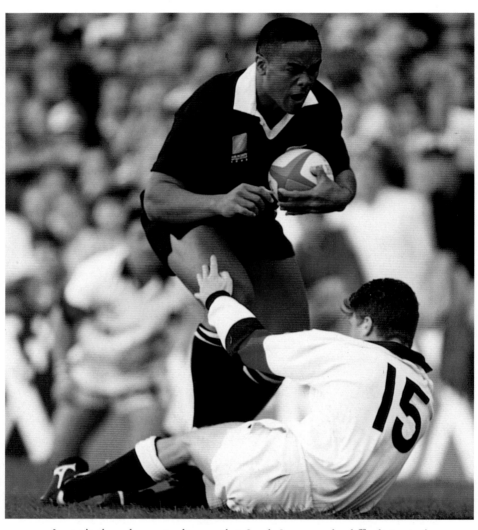

I wasn't the only one to discover that Jonah Lomu can be difficult to stop!
(David Rogers, Allsport)

I exhibit my customary poise under a high ball — and my desire to counter attack — during the Calcutta Cup game at Twickenham in March 1995 (David Rogers, Allsport)

Finding time for training, playing and touring isn't easy but an understanding employer makes life a little easier (David Rogers, Allsport)

My photograph for a magazine feature. Perhaps a modelling career beckons after my rugby career is over? (David Rogers, Allsport)

My collection of international jerseys grew rapidly during the World Cup
(Mike Holmes, Eastern Province Herald)

Country Club, before training again at 5 p.m. I had quite a good session, but people don't generally seem to be very happy with Jack Rowell at the moment.

We also got the chance to watch some tapes of Western Samoa games today – they're clearly going to be very hard to beat.

This evening I enjoyed a really pleasant meal at Langoustines restaurant just down the beach, a slap-up seafood meal. It was such a pleasure to hear all the old stories from Brian, Jason and the boys; the game has changed so much.

TUESDAY, 23 MAY

It's an official day off today, so I'm just about to go 'boogie-boarding' with television presenter Jim Rosenthal. I must admit I haven't been surfing like this for some time. It is so good to be back in sunny South Africa. A few members of the team have gone to play golf and others have gone to the township to do some coaching.

It's been brilliant so far but I'd love to let loose, have a few drinks, and really enjoy it. But I don't want to let anybody down, so it's one or two and then home to bed. This evening I went to the George and Dragon with Ben and Dewi, and met some fans from Bath. Then we went on to the Pig's Ear bar where we enjoyed some great South African hospitality. We were back safe in bed soon after midnight thanks to our security guards, who are being good fun as well. Two of them, Kelvin and Cassie, are brilliant guys. We know them from last year's England tour as they looked after us then as well. All of the guards are very professional at their job, and they need to be because we're surrounded by members of the public, and there's very little privacy unless you sit in your room all the time. I like having the supporters around, but sometimes it gets a bit overpowering when you just want some peace and quiet to sit, think, concentrate, and focus on your game.

WEDNESDAY, 24 MAY

There is so much tension in the camp I can hardly describe it. As our first match day draws closer, everyone is suddenly getting stroppy!

We had a two-and-a-half-hour training session this morning, which I think was uncalled for; Jack Rowell is in a panic as well as the team. Afterwards I did some kicking practice, before mooching off to have my hair cut. There was some good banter with the ladies in the hairdressing salon who were all insistent on telling me that South Africa would win the World Cup. I also had my first shave of the tour this morning, so I look a little more respectable.

This afternoon, myself, Kyran, Richard West and Neil Back went 'boogie-boarding' with the press corps who were keen to get us down to the sea to take some pictures. The waves were excellent.

We had a good meal in the Sports Café, but now everyone is in a shitty mood. All of a sudden there's no bounce in the camp, although myself and Tony Underwood always seem to see the funny side of things.

The funniest thing to happen so far is that John Mallett fell over in his shower and has pulled most of the tiles off his bathroom wall by accident. There is now a huge hole, and I mean a *huge* hole, in his bathroom wall. Otherwise it's very quiet. It's amazing how boring things get. All we seem to have done so far is play pool and watch videos of our opposition. My dad and Debbie are due to arrive soon so I've got something to look forward to.

THURSDAY, 25 MAY

Many of the fans have started to arrive in Durban now, and around 1,000 of them booked into our hotel last night! It's already a nightmare as far as privacy is concerned, but we've just got to cope with it.

The squad met to watch the opening game of the World Cup together, South Africa *v* Australia, and the consensus is that the Springboks were awesome.

The opening ceremony was a tremendous affair — a really exciting, inspiring occasion. It's wonderful to see the coloureds, blacks and whites all mixing together under the new national Rainbow flag. Rugby is uniting the nation, and I think that it has helped add to the country's excitement and interest in the tournament. I'm afraid I still get goose-bumps when they play the old South African national anthem, *Die Stem!* I suppose it's what I've grown up with.

A lot of the England players were very, very surprised about the outcome of the South Africa against Australia game. We had expected the Wallabies to win by 20 or more points, but while the Aussies looked dangerous when they got some momentum going, their backs were useless. The Springboks wanted it more, and the Springboks got it. I thought their half-back, Joel Stransky, was outstanding, and I think he will be one to watch for the rest of the tournament. Another is André Joubert. He blows hot and cold but he's a class player. I played with another Bok, Hennie le Roux, when I was in South Africa. Hennie played at centre for the Eastern Province B side when I was there.

We were all surprised to see David Campese dropping the ball and getting beaten; it just shows that it happens to the best of players, and it was a pleasure to see! But there's a long way to go, and I expect him and Michael Lynagh to play important rôles for the Wallabies in the rest of the cup matches.

The Springboks are obviously going to get a lot further than we thought. They are now going to have a relatively easy route through to the semi-finals, where they will probably play France or Scotland.

We all put R50 in the pot for a sweepstake on who would be the first try scorer, and Ian Hunter won the cash for betting on Michael Lynagh — he picked up R1,800 or £350, not a bad afternoon's work!

Before the game the boys sat out by the pool for a while and afterwards we went early-evening training at King's Park. The plan was that we were to have a closed session but the ground was full of celebrating South Africans. We trained well as a team today and everybody knew what they were doing. But, there's still a lot of niggle in the England camp – nerves, or that nasty medical condition, World Cup fever. I'm certainly looking forward to Saturday.

Having seen the boys in training, I think Jeremy Guscott could be one of the England players to watch – he loves being centre stage, world stage, and I think he's buzzing. He's got that arrogant side back to him again, for the first time in ages. Tim Rodber and Ben Clarke are training well, and will play key rôles in the team as I expected them to before we came, and so, too, will Brian Moore. Dewi Morris looks good, perhaps because he's been training very hard for the last six months, and he is very keyed up. It's unfortunate for Kyran that Dewi has got the scrum-half position for the Argentinian game, but I think the management has given Kyran an explanation; it's fair play for Dewi, who has done so much for English rugby.

Steve Ojomoh certainly seems to like the hard ground out here, although I prefer Deano in the side, if only because he's good under the high ball, and he gets back and helps me! Another one to watch this weekend is Rob Andrew. His kicking is immaculate at the moment. As for the back line, we are capable of a great deal, but it will all depend on how much ball we get. Hopefully, we won't struggle in the line-out department thanks to the mighty Martin Bayfield, and we'll get some clean, quick ball to the backs. Tony Underwood, Kyran Bracken and myself have got a lot to prove; a tournament like this can make or break you. We have got to keep our heads down and start performing.

I suspect that Jack Rowell will be looking for us to play the tactical game in the pool matches, and that he now intends to swop players around to keep them fresh. I think that he may rest Rob at some stage, play Jon Callard at full-back and kicker, and me at 10. I think that he may also rest Dewi for Kyran. With any luck we won't have an upset and lose one of the early games, which would be terrible, but anything can happen in this pressure cooker. Hopefully, we'll do well in the pool, and now I hope we meet Australia in the quarter-finals, because if they play like they did today we'll stuff them!

A few other things of interest today. According to the papers, the RFU has apparently announced that there is a £6-million deal for the players over the next four years, but as a committee member I know nothing about it. I was a bit flummoxed when the television reporters came round and asked me for a comment! None of us had even heard about it, and I don't even know whether it's true, so we'll have to see.

I went to another really good seafood restaurant today called Bailey's just outside Durban with J.C., Tony Underwood, Phil de Glanville, and Kyran. The food was superb, and we had a couple of bottles of wine while we relaxed into the evening.

It was Steve Ojomoh's birthday as well today, but luckily for him nobody found out.

FRIDAY, 26 MAY

Having seen the Springboks play yesterday, I'm itching for a game. I can hardly sleep at all now, and it's more tense than ever in the touring party, although I suppose that's understandable so close to a big game.

We were told to rest today. My dad flew in and it was good to see him. The wives and girlfriends, including my girlfriend, Debbie, arrive tomorrow. I hope it won't be too disruptive having them out here, although it's a great chance for them to be able to come over.

TWELVE

Learning to Swim in the Pool

SATURDAY, 27 MAY

Our first game is today, and we spent the morning sorting out one or two problems. The tension is overbearing, and there are camera crews everywhere.

• England *v* Argentina

After ten days' training and several months without a competitive game together, our first match was against Argentina at 5 p.m. this afternoon at King's Park, Durban. It's the only day we've been here so far where it's peed down with rain all day.

We went down to the stadium at about elevenish and kicked about. Because we were playing at 5 p.m. we had the whole day to sit around and it wasn't very nice. I think it's always very disruptive to play in the late afternoon, but we'll just have to adjust to later kick-offs because we have to play against the Samoans even later, at 8 p.m.

There wasn't anything like a full house at King's Park, and consequently there wasn't much of an atmosphere. It was so flat in the stadium that it didn't feel like a real World Cup game at all. But I still felt good in the run-up to kick-off and joined in singing the national anthem with gusto. However, it was a terrible performance by England, one of the worst for some years, and we could have lost to the Pumas who proved big, strong and full of initiative. The Argentinians nearly beat us. We were very jittery, and I can only assume the terrible tension finally got to us. Luckily, the boot of Rob Andrew kept us ahead in the match. We were 12–0 up at half-time, and I was relieved to see an Argentinian counter-attack come to nothing after I had failed to find touch with a kick from inside our 22.

Jack Rowell said we looked rusty at half-time and we knew it. Nothing had clicked, and nothing had worked. I thought I might have been the first England player on the scoresheet early in the second half, when I chased a kick from Rob Andrew into the left-hand corner, but it trickled into touch and that was it. In the end, we didn't score a try at all, and never looked like scoring, which made the bookies' odds of 9–2 on me scoring the first England touch-down against Argentina look decidely mean.

Two drop goals from Rob in the second half helped us keep our noses in front, although we were very worried when Argentina scored first in the fifty-fourth minute to make it 18–8, and then again at the death. Survival became the name of the game for us, and we trudged back into the changing-room after the game, dejected, even though we had won.

To a man we knew that we had not played up to our potential. Jack Rowell did not have to tell us that there was still a huge amount of work to do, and that vast improvements needed to be made. We knew that the class teams in the tournament like New Zealand would be chuckling to themselves contentedly and rubbing their hands together after our sub-standard performance.

Now, we have to get back to the drawing-board, and quickly. We had no control. Our scrummaging was loose and the ball we had was not quick enough, or clean enough. I think we missed the injured Dean Richards, who would have cleaned up a lot of that loose ball, especially in the line-out. But we can't make excuses; we were more frightened than frightening.

Jack Rowell said: 'We can only improve – otherwise we are going to go home faster than when we came out!' We know. Rob Andrew spoke for the team when he said we were 'appalling . . . very, very poor'. Rob added: 'We never got out of the blocks.' Luckily, he scored 24 points and we came through relatively unscathed. We eventually ran out 24–18 winners, although we were outscored two tries to nil. Everything that could have gone wrong did, and despite Rob's kicking, the Pumas could have scored a victory had they kicked their penalties. It was almost humiliating.

The Argentinians were very physical and their forwards played well. They were big strong guys and they dominated everything, and the crowd got behind them after about 20 minutes. I'm glad Ojo, and especially golden boot Rob Andrew had good games. But in many ways the Pumas deserved to win. They didn't allow us to play, and all credit to them. I didn't play too badly and I was steady under the high ball, but I did not get too many attacking opportunities. We didn't get quick enough ball, and I'll have to be patient.

It proved to us that we really have got a long way to go before we can even think about winning the World Cup. Skipper Will Carling seems to be okay about it all, but he also went off injured with bad bruising on his ankle and thigh, and he will miss the game against Italy on Wednesday.

It's a win, but there have been worrying signs tonight. It's as though we are thinking of the quarter-final already, not about getting to it, and that's dangerous. Hopefully things will get better. Surely they can only improve? I expect that Jack will make a couple of changes now for the next match against Italy (Kyran's sitting here with a smile on his face while I'm talking into my tape recorder). It's 9.01 p.m. and I'm off for a drink . . .

Footnote: It was a late night for the lads — or an early morning — and it was the first time we'd partaken of a drink or two. I had a few cane and Cokes, and it's just like drinking neat diesel!

Factfile: England 24 Argentina 18
- England scorers: Andrew, six penalties, two drop goals.
- Thanks to Rob Andrew England began the World Cup with a victory, the first time they have started the tournament with a win.
- Rob Andrew became the eighth player to reach 350 points in internationals.

What the press said

England insist they will never again put up such a gormless show.

THE GUARDIAN, 28 MAY 1995

SUNDAY, 28 MAY

We were training at 11 a.m. this morning and working off some of the frustration from yesterday's performance. We went over to the La Lucia Health and Racquet Club which has excellent facilities, and I did a bit of running, five minutes on the rowing machine and a few weights.

We had a good chicken lunch with family and friends, and it was good to see Debbie again. The boys were very pleased to see their wives and partners, and my dad was also there. A few mates came down to see me from Johannesburg. One other thing to celebrate today – it's John Mallett's birthday.

We had a team meeting at 7 p.m. and that's where it all came out. Jack sat us down and told us exactly what he thought of our performance against the Pumas, and what he expects in the next game. Jack said that Steve Ojomoh had played really well, but that he seemed the only one in the team who was committed to winning. I concede, we were definitely lazy. We'd trained hard enough, but we didn't pull it together for the game. Will spoke to us afterwards and we went through everything. He said we've got to watch ourselves otherwise we're going to be flying home sooner than we think.

I believe we took the field expecting that we were going to win, and you can't do that any more in international rugby these days. It would also help if we learned to relax and to enjoy our game a lot more. We've been very tense this week, and it hasn't helped. The tension may have had something to do with the fact that there has been very little to do in the hotel, and there are always so many supporters around all the time.

This evening, Debbie came over and we watched a video in my room.

MONDAY, 29 MAY

I got up and played golf with Jack Rowell, J.C. and Les Cusworth, and then we trained this afternoon at 5 p.m.

The golf was quite amusing. Jack doesn't tend to put a foot wrong in anything he does, and on the golf course it was the same. He took his time and always hit the ball about 120 yards straight down the fairway. He was very steady. On a typical hole the rest of us were in the rough about 300 yards away, despite the fact that J.C. and Les are normally quite tidy golfers. Jack took about four shots to get on the green, but it was all very impressive, and was a winning strategy. It was good to see him relaxing a little bit.

For some of the other boys it was even more entertaining. While Jerry Guscott, who plays off a low handicap of 12-ish, hit the ball straight down the fairway some distance, his fellow golfing partners, Jason Leonard and Bayf, were more erratic – Jason tended to play right down the left-hand side (in the rough), and Bayf played down the right-hand side (in the rough). Whenever these guys play together it's always quite a laugh, because it can take them about five hours to play nine holes!

TUESDAY, 30 MAY

Martin Johnson went 'boogie-boarding' today and the current's very strong out here, so much so that the lifeguard had to go out and get him back – all very amusing for his team-mates. Phil de Glanville also came a cropper in the sea. Phil had a red-raw stomach after the 'boogie-boarding' experience and none of us could understand why. That is, until we found out that he had been using the board upside down and resting on the rough polystyrene side. It instantly accounted for the severe chaffing of his tummy – again much to the amusement of the guys. Phil could well be awarded the Dick of the Day for his efforts.

Later on we went out for a very nice Japanese meal, where they cook everything in front of you. Ben had to rush off to see his girlfriend Michelle (again), before a few of the lads, including myself, went down to the ever-popular Joe Kool's where they were staging a topless mud-wrestling contest – surprise, surprise. J.C., Graham Dawe and the young Mike Catt only entered the establishment in question for a quick drink – honestly – to find three topless girls with one guy wrestling in all this mud and oil. But we only stayed for a couple of minutes. Too much excitement like that can't be good for you! Instead, we went back to the girls' hotel – not the mud wrestlers' I hasten to add – and had a couple of drinks there.

Rob Andrew has been made the captain for the Italy game which is good news for him. Rob has a 'little boyish' side to him and he is always full of jokes, so I expect he'll be chirpy for a while. Phil de Glanville is also selected to start in the team against Italy. Ojo's being rested, not dropped, but Victor is very disappointed that Jack has dropped him. Kyran Bracken will be playing in place of Dewi, and it will be good to see him producing the goods again.

Against Italy we'll be looking to swing the ball about and really get into the game. We need to score tries otherwise we could be in for a shock. If we lose a game, the winner of the group will be decided by the number of tries scored. We will have to do something about that tomorrow, as England and the Ivory Coast are the only teams not to have scored a try so far!

Will's okay now, and recovering from his knock; he's walking around with his cellular phone on his ear so he must be on the mend.

WEDNESDAY, 31 MAY

• **England v Italy**

Our second pool fixture at King's Park in Durban kicked-off at 5 p.m. this evening.

It was only the second time that we have played Italy and the last occasion was also in the World Cup, in 1991, when we beat them 36–6. This time around the margin of seven points in our 27–20 victory should have been much greater, but silly mistakes – one of them by me – made it look much closer than it was. I was involved in most of the tries in this game, one way or the other. I played a part in the two flying England touch-downs, and much to my horror and dismay, the first Italian try, just before half-time. The good news is that at least we now know we're in the quarter-final.

England's performance in wet and windy conditions was much improved compared to our effort against Argentina, but we still have a lot of work to do and we desperately need to improve before the match against Western Samoa on Sunday, and the quarter-final tie on 11 June. Our attitude was better in this game – some of the tension had gone – and there was more heart and commitment, but we're not playing as well as we know we can.

We had to soak up heavy Italian pressure in the first five minutes because they were very fired up. But we weathered the early storm, picked the ball up in our own 22 in broken play and mounted a superb counter-attack which ended with me passing to Tony Underwood. That felt good, and it was the first time in the tournament that I have had the chance to run into space. Tony raced down the wing and scored the first England try of the cup under the posts, and Rob converted to make it 7–0 after only eight minutes. It was just what we needed and should have been the springboard for much better things. It was certainly the start of a busy game for me!

When the rain started to come down a few minutes later, we went further ahead with another Rob Andrew penalty and, with the half-time whistle upon us, we had extended our lead to 16–3 courtesy of Rob's kicking. But with literally seconds to go before the break I took a catch deep in our 22 with the Italian forwards speeding towards me. I unwisely decided to kick into touch with my left foot, but didn't catch it properly. It was charged down by their number 14, Vaccarri, and the Italian scored. I was gutted – the first big mistake of my international career in a match in which we were desperate to impress. It took the score to 16–10 and needlessly put us under pressure. I pulled myself together at half-time, telling myself that the mistake would be my last of the World Cup, and the lads were very good about it in the dressing-room.

We scored another expansive try just after the break, with the other Underwood brother, Rory, scoring his first points of the campaign, having taken my pass and touched down in the corner. It took the score to 21–10 and then we should really have started pulling away and turning on the style, as it was the perfect chance for us to put things right on the field. But although we edged the score to 27–10, the Italians started to exert more pressure. First, I launched a desperate tackle to take out Properzi, who had broken away having intercepted a loose pass from Jerry Guscott – that put my pace to good use, because I thought he was away. And then Italy scored a converted pushover try at the end of the game, courtesy of Cuttitta, their captain, to make it 27–20 – too close for comfort against a team like Italy.

It's still a long way from where we want to be, and we need to be tighter in all areas, but it is an improvement. And we have to keep improving, and making less and less mistakes, if we are to have any chance of doing the business in this competition. Jack Rowell agrees. He told the press: 'It was a win and a clear improvement, but England lack the killer instinct. We are on an upward curve but only on the lower part.'

Factfile: England 27 Italy 20

- England scorers: R. Underwood, one try
                        T. Underwood, one try
                        Andrew, five penalty goals, one conversion

What the press said

Pedestrian England stuck on the road to nowhere.

DAILY TELEGRAPH, 1 JUNE 1995

THURSDAY, 1 JUNE

The day after the Italy game. We really wanted to go out and show everybody what we are capable of yesterday, but unfortunately it didn't happen again.

Personally, I felt very uncomfortable before the match. I was nervous, which is unusual for me, and nothing felt right. When my kick was charged down yesterday, it was one of the most demoralising things that has ever happened to me while I've been playing rugby. I kicked the ball with my head down and the first thing I knew was that it had hit someone. Then, when I turned around, the Italian was touching down. There were cameras flashing everywhere and the crowd was standing up and going crazy. I just thought, 'oh no!'. It was the first time that it has ever happened to me, and I felt terrible. But thankfully the team made a bit of a joke about it at the interval, which helped me, and I vowed not to kick off my left foot again.

I think I was fairly steady in the other aspects of my play. I wanted to get more involved and make up for my mistake, but I didn't get too much of an opportunity, although I was quite busy. It was all very disappointing. After the game last night we went out, had a couple of cane and Cokes and a singalong.

We're through to the quarter-final now and that's what we've all been waiting for. But before that, we've got to play against the big, tough Western Samoans on Sunday. Although the team hasn't been officially announced yet, there's a chance that I will be playing fly-half and J.C. full-back.

We spent this afternoon paint-balling, which can be even more dangerous than playing rugby – although one or two of my team-mates might not agree after two bruising encounters in just a few days. The forwards lay siege to the backs in all-out war, but many of the troops from both armies went AWOL, not fancying the fight. Those who stayed ended up more battered and bruised than after the game against Argentina! It was outstanding fun. We were all properly kitted out for battle. Myself and Phil de Glanville enjoyed ourselves as snipers on top of the roof of an old building, and some of our hits were even drawing blood. I was splattered three times in all and one of them, fired at me from quite a long way back, stung like anything.

The most amusing incident happened to Steve Ojomoh. He was lying on the floor concentrating on his shooting, and Kyran Bracken went up behind him and started pumping these paint pellets at his bum. It was hilarious and, as far as most of the lads are concerned, it has been the best social event of the tour so far.

We went out for another Japanese meal in the evening and the girls came along too. It all helped to take our minds off the rugby for a little while.

FRIDAY, 2 JUNE

There was a 5 a.m. call for team members keen to go shark spotting in the Indian Ocean, but I gave it a miss. It was just as well because reports back indicate that there was not a shark in sight after three hours at sea, only the guy who persuaded the mugs to get up early!

Today is an 'Activity Day' so there are a choice of pastimes including a flight in a Super Puma helicopter. I think there were 16 members of the team in the chopper and they told me it felt just like a scene out of Coppolla's movie *Apocalypse Now*. They also said that while they were flying up and down the coast, they passed over the hotel in which our girlfriends and wives are staying, and, apparently, they had GMTV's Mr Motivator in for a warm-up session. I would have loved to have gone on the helicopter ride but I missed it as my alarm didn't go off, so I played golf instead. Later on I did some kicking practice.

The team to play Western Samoa has been announced today and, as I thought, I'm playing at fly-half, which I don't mind, although I'll have to watch out as those Samoans are very large and very quick. I won't have a lot of time and I'll have to be careful with the charge down kicks! As well as playing one or two of the experienced team members who have been sitting on the bench,

Jack has called up a few of the keen young lads so that some our key players can be rested now that we're through to the quarter-final. J.C. will play at 15, Ian Hunter on the wing and Phil de Glanville at centre. Graham Rowntree and Graham Dawe have been called up and Richard West will get his first cap. Personally, I would have liked to have seen John Mallett and Damian Hopley start as well, and I think that they have both been a bit unlucky not to get the nod. Deano's still struggling, but I think he's going to be okay.

It's going to be a very hard match against the Samoans. I think Jack's in a bit of a panic about the game. He keeps on and on about winning on Sunday, although when you talk to some people from outside the camp they say that it wouldn't be too bad if we lost, as it would certainly mean an easier route to the final. But we don't go out to lose, so it's out of the question.

Rugby league was a major topic of conversation at supper. I've heard that two of the England players have already signed for rugby league next season, but I have not had it confirmed who they are!

SATURDAY, 3 JUNE

We had a really good training session this morning. There's a lot more enthusiasm in the side now that some of the younger players have been called in. They know what this game means for the team, and for themselves.

This afternoon we watched the French pip the Scots. The boys were delighted that the Scotland team were beaten, particularly as they lost it in the last minute! After the team meeting we also watched some of the South Africa v Canada game where the Springboks battered Canada into submission, with three players sent off in a stormy match. James Dalton was one of the three – he didn't go to Grey, but he played in the same competitions as I did back then, and even as a boy he was very tough. It was, nevertheless, an enjoyable game and the Canadians played really well, but it was a tough contest and will have tired the Springboks.

Tonight I went to see Mike and the Mechanics at the Village

Green in Durban with Deano, Brian, Dewi, Will and Julia, and some others. It was a brilliant concert and there was a good atmosphere. They finished about 11.30 p.m. and when they came back for their encore they came on in England jerseys! All the crowd went 'Booo!' but we thought it was great. (Later on in their tour, and ours, we went backstage and met Mike Rutherford and the band after their concert in Johannesburg, and they told us some entertaining stories. Unfortunately, they can't go into print!)

SUNDAY, 4 JUNE

Whatever happens today, it's our last day in Durban.

The All Blacks look awesome. We watched them score 145 points against Japan. With a bit more effort and extra training in ball skills I reckon that they could go far in this competition! Then we went off for our big game against Western Samoa. We understand that some people at home are still saying that we may throw this game so that we can play against South Africa in the quarter-final, instead of Australia, particularly as we have a very different team playing tonight. But nothing could be further from the truth. We want to win, and win well, which will be much better for the morale of the team. Before the game I had a chat to our team sports psychologist, Austin Swain — 'The Spook' — and he gave me some welcome reassurance.

• England v Western Samoa

This was our third game at King's Park, but tonight it was an 8 p.m. kick-off. We took on the mighty Western Samoans knowing that we had to play a great deal better than we played against Argentina and Italy, and it was our most convincing performance so far. We were all buzzing straight from the kick-off. With Rob Andrew out injured, I played at fly-half and really got into the swing of things for the first time in the tournament; a good early touch and safe kick helped me settle into the groove. Mentally, I found it very demanding playing at fly-half, but I think that I played quite well.

Playing with a heavily bandaged hamstring, Dean Richards gave us the instant fillip we needed, and within 90 seconds we had scored. Ojo won the ball at the back of a line-out and Victor burst through on the blind side. He found Dewi Morris, who had a terrific game, and when Dewi got stopped Neil Back went over for the try, his first for England.

Things went well for me. I put a few more good touch-kicks in, and one garryowen, before scoring my first points in the tournament after 26 minutes, with a flat close-range drop-kick which just bobbled over.

My England team-mates had been worried about my kicking; they needn't have bothered. Today it felt good. It must have also felt good for three of my Bath team-mates tonight. Jon Callard, who played at full-back, notched up 21 points as the stand-in kicker in the absence of Rob Andrew – five penalty goals and three conversions from nine attempts. Jon shows what talent we have on the England bench. Phil de Glanville had an excellent match again, and he must be pleased. And I was also delighted for another Bath buddy, John Mallett, who came on for his first cap after our prop, Graham Rowntree, limped off in this most physical encounter. John played really well in his début game, and when Damian Hopley came on for Will Carling in the second half and got his first cap, it meant that everyone in our squad had already played some part in the World Cup campaign.

With a few minutes to go before half-time, Rory Underwood scored a try from a move in which myself and Ian Hunter were involved, to give us a lead of 21 points. We felt high at half-time; we had fenced in the Western Samoans and there was more urgency and more control about our performance.

But after Fa'amasino's 40-metre penalty early in the second-half, we became a bit wobbly. For some reason we started very slowly. Replacement fly-half Fata Sini scored once, after a free kick, and then again, and our lead was suddenly cut to just seven points.

It was then that we showed our true mettle and dug in. After soaking up some pressure I was a key player in the move which led to us scoring a penalty try, when the Samoan forwards were caught well offside in attempting to stop us scoring. Then Rory scored his second smartly taken try of the game to take some of the pressure off; he's still a terrific finisher.

The whole mood of the camp is lifted by our victory, and I'm sure the Aussies won't fancy a quarter-final tie against us now, whatever David Campese might say. Our forwards were terrific tonight in one of the most physical contests I have ever played in.

In the few days leading up to the Argentina game we were tense and wound up. Things are much better now, and I think that it shows in our play – the teamwork tonight was much improved. There was pace and purpose about everything we did, and the spirit in the camp is much better. We are beginning to play as a team again. But there could be a downside after that bruising encounter; a hard night's work. It was a very physical game and Will, Tim Rodber and Deano all went off during the match. At this stage we don't need any serious injuries to our key players. Bring on the Wallabies (and the All Blacks) for the main event.

Factfile: England 44 Western Samoa 22

- England scorers: R. Underwood, two tries
  Back, one try. Penalty try
  Callard, three conversions, five penalties
  Catt, one drop-goal

What the press said

England will be delighted that at last they have scored a hatful of tries. Mike Catt's confidence at stand-off half was infectious and Dewi Morris, a bundle of energy at scrum-half, may have played his way into the side that will recreate the 1991 final.

Ojomoh soared at the back of a line-out, leaving the blind side clear for Ubogu to burst towards the line, find Morris in support and, when the scrum-half was stopped, Back squeezed his way over near the corner . . . It was just the start a reshaped XV required, while Catt welcomed an early touch of the ball with two raking clearances.

The back row, driven on by Richards, whose suspect hamstring was heavily bandaged, linked to good effect and gave Catt room to drop a low close-range goal.

DAVID HANDS, THE TIMES, 5 JUNE 1995

For the first time since arriving in South Africa, England, the Grand Slam champions, reminded the rest of the world that they, too, can present a genuine challenge in the knock-out stages of the competition . . .

It was the most physically demanding match I have ever seen.

Mike Catt, after an indifferent season as half-back for Bath, was a revelation at outside-half. The England backs knew they were going to get the ball and they responded well. But before this could happen there had to be control at the coal-face. It was here that England excelled, sending messages of warning to all remaining opponents.

JOHN MASON, DAILY TELEGRAPH, 5 JUNE 1995

Rowell might even have to think twice about where to play Mike Catt (against Australia). England's full-back was stuck in the No. 10 shirt against the Samoans and there was a zip about the back line which had been lacking beforehand. The form of Ian Hunter on the right wing was a bonus, but the deciding factor was that the England backs knew they were going to receive the ball from Catt instead of chasing kicks from Rob Andrew.

PAUL ACKFORD, DAILY TELEGRAPH, 5 JUNE 1995

[Mike Catt] did not seem to put a foot wrong . . . with solid touch-kicks relieving the pressure on England. He did equally as well in defence as in attack. He combined excellently with Dewi Morris, his half-back partner.

MICK SKINNER, THE SUN, 5 JUNE 1995

It will be a long time before England have such a talented group of individuals assembled together . . . We must aspire to see that talent released on the field.

JACK ROWELL, (WIDELY QUOTED SPEAKING AFTER THE GAME)

THIRTEEN

Clash of the Titans

On Sunday night after the game against Samoa, I went out with my brother and one of his mates. It was the first time we had really let loose and had a good night with a few tequilas.

MONDAY, 5 JUNE

We trained this morning. It's a long week and we don't want to burn ourselves out, so we are are going to do things in short, sharp bursts. We played football for a while, but that could have been a disaster on the injury front. Brian Moore should have been sent off for abusing the ref in the five-a-side tournament because he punched him! Martin Johnson also saw red when I tripped him up, and afterwards I had to get out of his way rather quickly.

I had a quiet lunch with my mother who was keen to catch up on my life and to tell me all the family news — I haven't seen her for ages. She's looking well and is very excited; she tells me that she is very proud.

This afternoon I went and played golf with Jerry, Phil de Glanville and Jon Callard. At the first tee I shanked it, and luckily nobody was in the way. My next shot was fine, but before I walked off in search of my ball I waited for J.C. to play his shot. I stood well out of the way, or so I thought, about three metres to the right of Jon and at quite an angle. But he still managed to slice the ball savagely into my hip. Thankfully, it didn't hurt at the time, and we all fell around laughing. It was so funny that Jerry ended up crying behind a tree, but I've got quite a bruise coming now! The golf wasn't too bad in the end — I only lost a couple of balls.

Later in the day, we set off for Johannesburg, our base for the rest of the tournament, whatever happens. Johannesburg is completely different from the sub-tropical beach resort of Durban. Situated inland, it is a big and dangerous city. Now we're at altitude, 6,000 feet above sea level, which literally brings new pressures and challenges. It's much harder catching your breath, let alone the ball, and you can find yourself gasping for air. Thankfully, we're not playing in Johannesburg for the time being. We're playing our quarter-final, and our semi-final match when we make it through, in Cape Town. We'll just fly down and back for the game(s). We will, therefore, only have to play one game here in Johannesburg, the final at Ellis Park! The Aussies are staying here, too, so we're not out on a limb.

The injury list after last night's game against Western Samoa looks worrying. Neil Back has a hamstring injury, and prop Graham Rowntree is also crocked with a pulled calf muscle. My room-mate, Kyran Bracken, has had an injured heel since the Italy game and it is possible he may have to go home.

It will be tough for Jack to pick the team against Australia. Phil de Glanville, in particular, has played really well when he's stepped in for Will or Jerry Guscott, and it will be hard on him if he is omitted in favour of Jerry for the game against the Wallabies. Jerry was rested against the Samoans. Jack told the papers: 'Obviously, if you have three centres fighting it out it's better than two. It's a great opportunity for Phil. Certain senior players have been a bit complacent.' That's Jack's confrontational style all over.

TUESDAY, 6 JUNE

Training and waiting. The tension is starting to build again.

WEDNESDAY, 7 JUNE

The team is announced for Sunday's game against the Wallabies and I'm restored to the full-back position. Phil de Glanville has missed out and Jerry's back in the team. I feel sorry for Phil; he's played so well when he's been given the chance. I know that Jerry met with Jack Rowell to discuss the situation before the team was announced, and I understand that Jerry told Jack how he saw us playing on Sunday and what his rôle could and would be. So it will be Carling and Guscott against Horan and Little, which should be a terrific clash.

Will, I know, sees Jerry as a key to unlocking the Wallabies' defence. 'Jerry has an ability very few players possess and, as a team, we have to pull out a big performance.' Will also said that the England team always seems to rise to this kind of challenge — it brings out the best in the squad. He thinks it will be a closely fought game, but he is confident that we can beat Australia.

Jack Rowell has said that he wants big games from us all this weekend, and he'll get what he wants — we feel good, and the mood is very positive (as well as very sober in our no-drink zone). The only change from the victorious Grand Slam team is that Dewi is in at scrum-half for Kyran.

The injury list looks a little better, with Graham Rowntree and Neil Back on the mend. Kyran's heel is still causing problems and there has been some talk of a replacement flying out from home.

It's bad luck for the guys who played so well against Western Samoa but have not made it into the team to take on the Aussies. However, I'm sure that the team Jack has picked has it in them to overturn the defeat in the 1991 World Cup final. If Brian Moore's determination is anything to go by, revenge will be sweet. We want to stay in the World Cup, and to do that we have to win on Sunday. So that's what we're going to do.

THURSDAY, 8 JUNE AND FRIDAY, 9 JUNE

The tension is sky high. A whole week really is a long time to wait for the quarter-final at this stage of the competition. We want to get on with it, and waiting simply puts everyone on edge, although training is going well and everything seems to be coming together at just the right time.

My dad and oldest brother are coming to watch the game on Sunday — the first time my dad has ever seen me play in a full international. I hope we put on a good performance for him.

The England team is ready for Australia, having rediscovered our self-confidence, and I expect us to win many of the 'personal battles' on the pitch on Sunday, especially among the forwards and at the line-outs. We all think it will be close, and know we will have to play at the top of our game to beat the Wallabies.

Tim Rodber's clash with Willy Ofahengaue will be a big one and so, too, will Deano's against Tim Gavin. Ben Clarke against the Aussie open-side flanker David Wilson will also be a good match. If we can win control in these contests, then we will have a platform for Rob Andrew and the backs to go on and win the game. We must stop the Australians getting clean ball. We don't want Campo to get a look in and, after all he has said, we're determined to keep him out of the game!

I know that Jack Rowell has every confidence in us. He thinks we're a talented squad, but he says that now we've got to 'release' that talent on the field; the team knows it too. The England efforts in the World Cup seem to have caught the imagination of the country back home, just like in South Africa, and we want to win for the country as well as ourselves. We will not contemplate defeat this weekend. We've waited four years to get our own back in a big World Cup game and we are all determined that the Aussies will be going home on the first plane on Monday morning.

We went go-karting which was great fun and helped us to let off some steam. The 'dream-team' of Will, Rory, Rob and myself had one of the fastest cars, and we were well in the lead until all of the other teams ganged up on us. It ended up with Will giving Kyran a thump for bumping us off the track so that we couldn't race anymore. It was quite a good way of getting rid of some of the pent-up tension.

SATURDAY, 10 JUNE

We're now in Cape Town ready for tomorrow's game against the Australians and we spent the afternoon watching France overcome Ireland 36–12. Then we saw South Africa give a superb display of controlled rugby against the strong Western Samoans, beating them 42–14. South Africa's 'Black Pearl' from Cape Province, winger Chester Williams, made South African rugby history by becoming the first player to score four tries in an international for his country – in only his first game of the tournament. Chester was involved in the build-up to the fourth try he scored, before finishing it off – a fairytale for him, and for every black African in South Africa. Those tries can do nothing but further South African unity. It was a marvellous performance, although the Springbok injury list will probably look a bit like ours did after the game against the Southsea islanders, following some really late tackles, particularly on van der Westhuizen.

I had expected the tension would get to the Springboks and that they would struggle to beat the Australians in the opening game of the tournament. But winning that crunch match gave them, and the South African people, an incredible morale boost, and they are now playing as if they are invincible. The South African people clearly expect the Springboks to win the cup, and nothing less will do. The return of Chester Williams, recovered from injury, has given the Springboks an added lift, and his performance against the Samoans has entirely justified the incredible hype that surrounds the team's only black player. South Africans everywhere are now on a high. France will struggle to hold them in the semi-final.

Our sports psychologist, Spook Austin Swain, gave everyone in the squad a sheet of paper today, with slips numbered 1 to 21. The orders were that we had to fill in comments about every other player on each of the slips, positive comments and no jokes. All the results were collected up and then put in personalised envelopes, and posted under everybody's door ready for us to read before bed. Receiving those slips of paper full of positive comments about me from my team-mates did wonders for my confidence, and for everybody else's, I think. It was a great boost for all of the players in tomorrow's game.

SUNDAY, 11 JUNE

• **England v Australia**

The quarter-final of the 1995 World Cup at Newlands, Cape Town, 12 noon.

ENGLAND

15	M.J. Catt (Bath)
14	T. Underwood (Leicester)
13	W.D.C. Carling (Harlequins)*
12	P.J.C. Guscott (Bath)
11	R. Underwood (Leicester)
10	C.R. Andrew (Wasps)
9	C.D. Morris (Orrell)
1	J. Leonard (Harlequins)
2	B.C. Moore (Harlequins)
3	V.E. Ubogu (Bath)
4	M.O. Johnson (Leicester)
5	M.C. Bayfield (Northampton)
6	T.A.K. Rodber (Northampton)
7	B.B. Clarke (Bath)
8	D. Richards (Leicester)

AUSTRALIA

15	M. Burke (New South Wales)
14	D.P. Smith (Queensland)
13	J.S. Little (Queensland)
12	T.J. Horan (Queensland)
11	D.I. Campese (New South Wales)
10	M.P. Lynagh (Queensland)*

* captain

9	G.M. Gregan (ACT)
1	D.J. Crowley (Queensland)
2	P.N. Kearns (New South Wales)
3	E.J.A. McKenzie (New South Wales)
4	R.J. McCall (Queensland)
5	J.A. Eales (Queensland)
6	V. Ofahengaue (New South Wales)
7	D.J. Wilson (Queensland)
8	B.T. Gavin (New South Wales)

Referee: D.J. Bishop

I was so nervous before the game that I drank some coffee and then puked it up, but once we took the field it all went very well. In fact, this was undoubtedly the game of my life, and I can't imagine ever playing in a match again which is so tense, so close, and so exciting. There were tears in the changing-room afterwards and some of the players were singing a song specially for the Aussies; I think it's called 'Leaving on a Jet Plane'.

To win as we did, in injury time at the end of the game, was extraordinary; to do it against the world champions in the shadow of Table Mountain made it even more special.

Once we had clawed the score back to 22–22 with a few minutes to go, we knew that if we could force the Wallabies back into their half we were in with a chance – if we got clean ball. With 20 minutes extra time looming, we won a penalty and Will Carling threw the ball to me to kick for touch. I'd been kicking well out of hand, but I instantly knew this was the big one. I just kept my head down as Dave Alred (the kicking coach) had said. If I sliced it, I thought my career would be over. Luckily, I hit it well and it landed near their ten-metre line. I had successfully completed the first stage.

Rob Andrew later told *The Sun*:

'From the moment Mike Catt struck such a beautiful penalty kick to touch on Australia's 22-metre line I knew a drop-goal was the best option . . . If he had missed, it would have been awful because Australia would have had the chance to run the ball back at us. If he had found a shorter touch, it would have made the drop-goal that much more difficult. But he hit a pearler!'

And match-winner Rob told Michael Calvin of *The Daily Telegraph*:

'Deano and I talked about what we might do as we walked to the line-out. We had a couple of options. I could put the ball up to the sticks or drop the goal. It was a great catch by Bayf, then the forwards did the damage. They drove in-field, committing the back row, and giving me that little bit more room.'

As Rob said, the game-plan worked to perfection; the move from the line-out was straight out of the rugby union textbook. Martin Bayfield took a wonderful catch in the line, the pack drove on a few metres, and the ball came out cleanly to Rob from Dewi Morris. He had the space and time, and just enough energy, to send a towering drop-kick through the posts from fully 45 yards. Rob's face was a picture after he dropped that goal.

The catch from Martin Bayfield, who had a mighty contest with his Aussie counterpart, John Eales, was magnificent, and the kick, beyond words. 'I'd hit it from so far out. The wind was taking it to the right, but it was comfortably inside,' said Rob.

I can't remember being so happy, so full of adrenalin. And when we came off it was just as if we had won the cup itself, for it felt like a cup final and was surely worthy of a billing as the decider to the Webb Ellis Trophy. What a shame it wasn't the final! It was certainly the game of the tournament, so far, and perhaps one of the best games ever.

David Campese was the first to shake Will Carling's hand on the pitch and somebody even filmed Dennis Easby kissing and hugging Will on their video recorder after the game! Jack Rowell said: 'When I see the RFU president in tears, kissing the captain, I know we've made a huge impact! This has been a big day for England; not for England rugby, for England.'

Coming into the quarter-final match I had never been beaten in an England jersey, and I was determined that today wasn't going to be my first defeat as a full international. We were fired up beyond belief and the tension was unbearable before we went on to the pitch. But we were focussed on the job in hand, and we felt good; training had gone superbly well all week. I think we could feel it coming together just at the right time. But we all knew that there was no room for error, and last night Jack drummed it into us that today was our only bite of the cherry. He said that we could not meet again on Monday to put things right, if we lost.

It was cold, wet and windy at Newlands, and within seconds of the start Deano got a nasty bang on the head and had to go off for running repairs. He came back on again, and again, and again — despite needing seven stitches — and had a big game in all respects. What a player for his country. But, of course, he wasn't the only one — so many of the team had the game of their lives.

I took an early high catch after a couple of minutes and ran the ball into touch, which gave me a good feel of the ball, and I was busy all afternoon with up-and-unders from Michael Lynagh and Campo.

While Dean Richards was off for the first time, we conceded a silly penalty and Lynagh made it 0–3 — just what we didn't want early on. Shortly afterwards I got my second high ball of the match; if I had got off lightly in the Five Nations, I've really been tested in South Africa, with more high balls than I care to remember!

It was 3–3 after five minutes when the Aussie backs were penalised and Rob Andrew kicked the first three of his 20 priceless points. A few moments after that we took the lead for the first time, when Rob fired in a monster penalty from the right-hand touchline — the perfect way to punish Australian foul play.

Ten minutes gone and I took a real pressure catch from a huge, high, Michael Lynagh kick — three safe ones in the first ten. It was clearly going to be a testing game for me, and I had the feeling that the Aussies must have decided in training that my catching was a weak point for them to attack. But so far I was holding my own really well and had no intention of letting the Aussies get the better of me.

When Tony Underwood scored our try in the twentieth minute, I was on cloud nine. Michael Lynagh made an unforced handling error in our half, and Rob Andrew's quick hands fed Jerry Guscott, who passed a great ball to Will. He timed and weighted his pass superbly to Tony, who ran like the wind up the touchline to score. I was chasing up behind him at full speed, waving my arms frantically, egging him on and shouting 'Go on! Go on, Tony!' at the top of my voice and punching the air. It must have helped, because he evaded a couple of desperate tackles before touching down. I was celebrating even before he scored, because I knew he was going over! Rob converted the try and suddenly we were in control, 13–3 ahead. It was at that point that we knew we could win the game, the important thing now was to keep up the pressure. We seemed to be controlling the line-outs, and our forward play was awesome. Everything was going exactly as we had planned and the Wallabies were under severe pressure to stay with us, and stay in the game.

The high kicks continued to come my way and before half-time I took another three awkward catches cleanly under pressure. I was beginning to feel that this was going to be my day!

Lynagh missed a big penalty kick in front of the posts from a long way out, shortly before the turn-around. He scored another right on half-time to make it 13–6, after Deano was caught offside. However, had the Aussies gone in at 13–9 – playing like they did in the second half – it could have been a different story in the end.

It was 13–6 at the break, and with 40 minutes to play we were in no doubt that we were about to play the most important half of our careers, so far. For some reason unknown to us, we had taken our foot off the accelerator pedal for a few minutes before the interval, and we were still at half speed after the restart. Within seconds of half-time a brilliant high kick from Lynagh was coming down with ice on it, right towards me. I steadied myself for the catch, and Tony Underwood was right there with me, but Wallaby Damian Smith appeared from nowhere, steaming in at pace. He jumped high, caught the ball and rolled over to score. Myself and Tony didn't have a chance and we were all stunned.

All our good work in the first half had suddenly evaporated to nothing. Looking back, it was a truly great try, and it meant that the Aussies were right back in the game – indeed, they were now in the driving seat. Lynagh converted to make it 13-all, and with the Wallaby tails up, some of our critics may have already written us off. But Rob slotted another penalty to make it 16–13 after 46 minutes and the game began to see-saw. If it was nerve-wracking to play in, it must have been hell to watch! England conceded another daft penalty for being offside defending at a ruck two minutes later, and Lynagh kicked the Aussies level again.

The game had completely turned around at the half-time break. The worry for us was that now the Wallabies were having all the ball, and we were losing the line-outs on our own throw-ins. The forward dominance we had showed in the first half had all but disappeared. The Australians had come right back, and were now on top.

Another garryowen was sent up for me – it must have been a team decision to send everything my way – and I took another safe catch. But then we gave yet another penalty away! Rob equalised straight away in the sixtieth minute after the Aussies were penalised for obstruction; 19-all.

There was no pause for breath. Lynagh kicked another penalty to make it 19–22 after Tim Rodber was somewhat harshly penalised for holding, and then Rob missed a kick from halfway on 65 minutes. When I missed a drop-goal chance with a horrible flat and mis-directed kick with five or so minutes to go, I felt, for the first time, that the game might have slipped away from us.

But the lionheart spirit was big, and somehow Rob scored a penalty with four minutes left to tie-up the scores again at 22–22. The tension was even more unbearable than before the game. With just one minute left on the clock we were terrified about conceding a penalty from a Wallaby scrum in front of our posts and, if we didn't, we thought that Lynagh would probably have a go for a drop-goal. But he didn't and the forwards drove into us and tried to dent our defences. That may have cost them the game because we cleared downfield from my penalty kick, and Rob scored his eighty-third-minute winning drop-goal that put the world champions out, and on the plane back home. I had promised to put them on that plane and now they're getting their tickets ready. We felt elated afterwards, mentally and physically drained. But so high.

I heard Will comment to the television cameras: 'I've never played in anything like that. It was a great game.' He also told the cameras that we had known we had to get the ball into their half at the end of the game, and put pressure on the Australians. 'It was a huge effort,' he said. It was.

Rob was virtually speechless when they interviewed him; drained. Like the rest of the squad, he could hardly believe it. We had nearly been dead and buried by the Aussie pressure in the second half, pinned right back on our heels, and starved of good quality clean ball. In fact, we were starved of possession altogether after the break, and it showed why the Wallabies are a great side – still a great side. We didn't collapse under the pressure, however, and we toughed it out and came back to take the game, which makes us something special, too. To win as we did was unbelievable. Rob delivered, and we have proved to everybody, ourselves included, that we are right up there with the very best teams in the world. I should think this was one of England's greatest performances ever.

The dressing-room was in shock after the game; a mixture of shock, jubilation and complete exhaustion. It had been so tense, and yet Aussie coach Bob Dwyer said that he didn't find the game as exciting as 'some other ways to play'. He should have been out there! The England boys are in total agreement with our boss Jack Rowell who retorted: 'That's one of the matches of all time, as far as I'm concerned. There were two giants out there.'

Now we're on a roll and our confidence is high. If we can beat the Wallabies, we can take New Zealand, victors 48–30 over Scotland. We just need to rest, and recover from the excitement, to recharge our mental as well as our physical batteries.

Despite the team's self-imposed alcohol ban, I think we might have a little gargle tonight! I still haven't been on a losing England side and I hope my luck stays with me. Congratulations also to Brian Moore, for him revenge has been so sweet. He can now retire a happy man, if he wants to. No such luck for Campo.

After the exhausting game we went to Bertie's Landing for dinner with the girls, which was fun, and then we went on to the Sports Café which was packed with England supporters. 'Swing Low Sweet Chariot' was the order of the day.

Factfile: England 25 Australia 22

- Scorers: T. Underwood, one try

    Andrew, five penalties, one conversion, one drop-goal

- Rob Andrew's 20 points took his World Cup tally to 61 points. He has now scored 227 points out of England's total of 393 in the last 13 games.

What the press said

Mike Catt had a resplendently assured game.

FRANK KEATING, THE GUARDIAN, 12 JUNE 1995

I have criticised England full-backs for not catching those bombs before they bounce and for having shoulders like an Aspirin bottle. But, I've got to admit, I like this one. The crafty Catt. This pretty boy can attack as well. He looks comfortable on the ball — 9/10.

MICK SKINNER, THE SUN, 12 JUNE 1995

Nobody performed with greater finesse than Mike Catt at full-back. He was brilliant and brave in the face of the on-rushing Aussie avalanche — and his handling and kicking were faultless.

ROGER UTTLEY, WRITING IN THE DAILY MIRROR, 12 JUNE 1995

[Mike Catt] was faultless under the high ball, even though Damian Smith out-jumped him to snap up the Aussie try. Few chances to attack, but great positional sense − 8/10.

'HOW THEY RATED', THE DAILY MIRROR, 12 JUNE 1995

[Mike Catt] Superb throughout . . .

TODAY, 12 JUNE 1995

When I see the RFU president in tears, kissing the captain, I know we've made a huge impact! This has been a big day for England; not for England rugby, for England.

The dressing-room is full of very emotional and tired young men who have done their country proud.

That's one of the matches of all time, as far as I'm concerned. There were two giants out there.

JACK ROWELL, SPEAKING AFTER THE GAME

We did our best but it wasn't good enough. The England defence was too strong.

AUSTRALIAN CAPTAIN MICHAEL LYNAGH, SPEAKING TO THE DAILY MAIL, 12 JUNE 1995

One of the many images to linger in the mind from the climactic Rugby World Cup quarter-final between England and Australia was that of an ecstatic English trio captured on celluloid as they left the field: Will Carling, Tony Underwood, Mike Catt. As marketable a group of English players as you could wish for.

DAVID HANDS, THE TIMES, 14 JUNE 1995

FOURTEEN

Beaten Black and Blue

MONDAY, 12 JUNE

I'm very happy and not too hung-over. There were some very sore heads when we went over to Sun City for rest and recuperation, courtesy of the RFU. Sun City means sunshine, artificial beaches, water slides, a massive – unbelievable – wave machine, the Lost City, a superb golf course, and no-holds barred extravagance. It is an awesome place. I lost £300 in the casino today, and I'm one of many. Only Jerry and Damian have won anything at all.

TUESDAY, 13 JUNE

I got up early and played nine holes of golf at the Lost City with Tony and Jerry. It was not the best of days for my golf. Then we went down to the magnificent water slides, which have to be seen to be believed; you can't see where the hell you're going in them. There is also a wave pool, and a lake for skiing, para-sailing, and anything else to do with water sports. Five of us had a go on a banana before trying virtually everything else on offer, including para-sailing. If parachuting is like that, then I want to do it!

I was really tired and I fell asleep in the bath. After dinner we went to see the Sun City Extravaganza show before going to the casino to try and win our money back. We didn't, and I lost some more. I'm now down R1,900. I'll have to stop . . .

WEDNESDAY, 14 JUNE

We have arrived back at our hotel in Sandton, Johannesburg, to prepare for the big game at the weekend. We're feeling confident now. New Zealand aren't anything special and we think we have the ability to beat them. Whether we do or not is another matter, and will depend on our performance. We know we're in the top four teams in the world, but want to go the whole way.

Thanks to the excellent Sun City trip we are relaxed again after the game against Australia. You can't believe how much a game like that takes out of you mentally. We were like dead zombies after it, 100 per cent mumbo!

THURSDAY, 15 JUNE AND FRIDAY, 16 JUNE

Training and relaxing. David Campese is still giving England a hard time, even though his Australian team are out of the competition. Campo wants the All Blacks to beat us on Sunday because of the England style of play. 'The future of rugby is at stake,' he told Chris Jones of *The Evening Standard* back home in England. 'Imagine England and South Africa getting through to the final. Why would you go and watch rugby if those two were fighting it out to be world champions?'

He must be bitter about losing last weekend, and playing out of form, but we don't care! As far as I am concerned, it doesn't matter how we beat New Zealand, as long as we win. With Rob in such great kicking form, we haven't needed to run the ball so far in the tournament. But if the All Blacks start getting the upper hand and taking control, then it will be another matter. It's win at all costs for us this Sunday, and whatever style we end up playing, we want that victory.

Many of the England side played in the winning team against the All Blacks in 1993, but I didn't. Now I want my turn! When we beat the All Blacks 15–9 at Twickenham, it was a watershed. It showed us that the New Zealanders are not invincible, although we certainly won't be complacent, and once again we'll have to better our performance against the Wallabies if we are going to win.

Our battle with the massive, flying Jonah Lomu will be one of the key clashes. But, if Deano, Tony and everyone else fail, I reckon I can bring the 6 ft 5in, 18½ stone wing down – chicken feed! I suspect he won't get a chance to run at me, because we'll have him under so much pressure that he won't get a look in, and we know that there are big chinks in his defensive game. A few well-positioned balls in behind Mr Lomu from Rob and myself, and we'll see how good he is, and how quick he can turn that huge frame. If you get the All Blacks on the back foot, anything can happen; the Scots and the Japanese scored tries against them, and so can we. We want to win this game even more than the one against Australia, and the All Blacks are in for a surprise.

As well as loads of videos of the All Blacks in action, we have also had the inside track on how to beat them from some of the friendly Australian players who we saw at Sun City earlier in the week. They kindly gave us the benefit of their vast experience at toppling the boys in black. Many of them think we can do it if we carry on believing in ourselves. I think the real reason that most of the Aussies are keen for us to win is that they can't stand the thought of the All Blacks winning the cup, and rubbing their noses in it for the next four years.

We intend to take them on and beat them up front, with the line-out plays crucial. We need to keep the ball in our hands, put the All Blacks under pressure and tot up points on the board to get them rattled. If we can play as we did against Australia for the first 20 minutes, and then try and sustain that level of commitment and intensity, we'll win. Then we'll see about throwing the ball about and turning on the style.

Rob has been awarded the MBE in the Queen's Birthday Honours List, so he was relentlessly teased all day. Rob says it's an honour for the whole team and for rugby union, but I know he'd rather have the Webb Ellis Trophy in his hands next weekend.

The build-up to this game has gone quickly, perhaps because we had a couple of days off. There were three nominations for Dick of the Day today, Friday: Brian Moore for playing his cymbals in the bus, Graham Dawe, who ran out of hair gel and used shaving cream, and Dewi — just for being Dewi, I think. Brian Moore won on the clapometer.

In the afternoon we went down to Cape Town to get ready for the match. Richard, Douglas, and my mum and dad are all coming down to watch the game. This evening we relaxed by watching the movie *Bad Boys*.

SATURDAY, JUNE 17

We've gone into a new hideaway training venue because too many watchful eyes are on us.

This afternoon we watched the Springboks just beat the French in really terrible weather conditions in Durban — I've never seen anything like it down there — but they only just managed the victory, and we all thought the French had scored near the end.

After the Spook's really clever ploy to get us hyped up by writing morale boosting things about each other before the game against the Aussies last weekend, I'm looking forward to seeing what he comes up with for tonight.

SUNDAY, JUNE 18

In the end Spook Swain just sat us down together and we went through what each of our jobs would be on the field today, and how we were going to go about those tasks. It helped to focus our minds, and, at this stage, everything is welcome as we know it's going be a tough afternoon.

• England *v* New Zealand
At last, the semi-final at Newlands, Cape Town, kick-off 2 p.m.

ENGLAND

15	M.J. Catt (Bath)
14	T. Underwood (Leicester)
13	W.D.C. Carling (Harlequins)*
12	P.J.C. Guscott (Bath)
11	R. Underwood (Leicester)
10	C.R. Andrew (Wasps)
9	C.D. Morris (Orrell)
1	J. Leonard (Harlequins)
2	B.C. Moore (Harlequins)
3	V.E. Ubogu (Bath)
4	M.O. Johnson (Leicester)
5	M.C. Bayfield (Northampton)
6	T.A.K. Rodber (Northampton)
7	B.B. Clarke (Bath)
8	D. Richards (Leicester)

NEW ZEALAND

15	G. Osborne (N Harbour)
14	J. Wilson (Otago)
13	F. Bunce (N Harbour)
12	W. Little (N Harbour)
11	J. Lomu (Counties)
10	A. Mehrtens (Canterbury)
9	G. Bachop (Canterbury)
1	C. Dowd (Auckland)
2	S. Fitzpatrick (Auckland)*
3	O. Brown (Auckland)
4	I. Jones (N Harbour)
5	R. Brooke (Auckland)
6	M. Brewer (Canterbury)
7	J. Kronfeld (Otago)
8	Z. Brooke (Auckland)

Referee: S. Hilditch

* captain

Before the game, David Campese told the television audience that
the result would depend on who got the better of the line-out,
and Gavin Hastings said that it would be won or lost up front.
Both thought it would be a close call. Only Gareth Edwards got
it right when he said that if the All Blacks won ball, England would
be in trouble. They did, and we were, right from the kick off.

England were on the rack from the start. To our surprise,
Andrew Mehrtens switched the direction of his kick away from his
forwards towards man-mountain Jonah Lomu. The switch threw
us, and we were off balance for the rest of the first half. It was a
move the All Blacks had apparently planned six months ago,
correctly guessing that we would be their opponents in today's
semi-final. They deliberately broke up our pattern of play, taking
the ball away from our forwards, and in those opening moments
we were nowhere. Tony Underwood and Will collided, and
between them fumbled the ball. The resulting knock-on summed
up much of our play for the afternoon, and before we knew it the
bionic man Lomu had run in an unstoppable try, followed quickly
by another one from Josh Kronfeld. After six minutes we were
12–0 down, and the game had already slipped out of our grasp.

We were completely shell-shocked, almost like rabbits startled
in the headlights of an approaching car – driven by that 20-year-
old Lomu. We had thought his inexperience would tell; it didn't.
Rob Andrew had said before the game that Lomu was already the
player of the tournament. 'We'll have to make sure we put him
on the floor,' he said, but, on the day, we came nowhere near
downing him, and he ran in four tries in the All Blacks' 45–29
victory – the most points ever conceded by an England team.

That first try Lomu scored was extraordinary. After the New
Zealand scrum the ball came down the line to Lomu, but it was
passed behind him – the game plan was obviously to get the ball
moved wide to Lomu as quick as possible. The ball was bouncing,
and he was off balance, unable to pick it up at pace. But he still
managed to beat off Tony Underwood's first attempt at stopping
him, and then he went past Will, leaving me as the last line of
defence. I set myself for the tackle and, as far as I was concerned,

I was well set when I took him – or tried to take him – but just as he did to Gavin Hastings in the All Blacks game against Scotland, he ran straight through me to score. I tried to get his waist, to go in low, but it was no good. I remember lying on the ground feeling as if I had been run over by a steamroller, and he also whacked me with his boot on the way. It was as if he was smiling when he went past me, which was doubly annoying. He was always giving those little smiles; it was disconcerting. I felt like I was the fall-guy in a Tom and Jerry cartoon. As I was struggling to my feet, Frank Bunce ran by and said, 'Have some of that then!'

The All Blacks were very verbal throughout the game. It was much the same story for their second try. As I was on the ground, New Zealander Ian Jones came over and said, 'Have some fucking more of that, then!'. And when I kicked for touch a few minutes later, the first time I had really got my hands on the ball, All Blacks' captain Sean Fitzpatrick ran past and shouted over to me, 'Whatever happened to the running game, chickenshit?'. It was a shame that we didn't do much on the field so we could have a go back.

Lomu has already been offered a whole host of deals to become a rugby league player. I hope he goes, and goes quickly. As Jack Rowell commented, someone should have bought him up before the World Cup! I don't think that we realised his power until too late. Last night, before the game, I was playing cards and Graham Dawe was watching a video of the All Blacks *v* Scotland tie. When I glanced over I saw Lomu boshing Gavin Hastings, and my first thought was 'Shit, Gavin must be at least three stone heavier than me.' And that's how it was for the whole of the game. He ran through us as if we were not there, with huge power and speed, and it wasn't just me he boshed. Tim Rodber lined him up and tried to pin him, but Lomu ran over him, laughing. Then Martin Johnson had a go and he did the same thing. Lomu tackled Ben Clarke from behind, and Ben says it's the hardest tackle that he has ever taken. Poor old Tony Underwood had a bad time against him as well, but you can't single out any one person in the team for blame. It was down to all of us, me included. The man is a giant and perhaps we underestimated him. There's already a joke doing the rounds. Did you know that the RSPCA is looking for Jonah Lomu? Why? Because he ran over a Catt!

We were stunned, but even then there may have been a way back had we taken one or two of our chances. Rob missed a drop-goal chance, for once in his life, and a couple of first half penalties, which may have kept us in touch. But the fact was that we couldn't stay with the All Blacks. Mehrtens notched up another penalty after 11 minutes to make it 15–0, and then the New Zealand number eight, Zinzan Brooke, kicked a towering drop goal to make it 18–0, worthy of any world-class fly-half. After 25 minutes Jonah Lomu left Rob for dead, and it was 25–0 after the try was converted. To all intents and purposes, the game was over. We were blitzed in that opening, in a way I have never experienced before. The only way we could stop the All Blacks was to have the ball, but they had it, and wouldn't give it back except for kick-offs, for the opening quarter and more!

With half an hour gone, and no points on the board, we had our first hopeful break, but Rob dropped the ball when we had a four to three overlap. What a difference a week makes.

When Jack Rowell came on to the pitch at half-time our only score had been a late penalty to make it 25–3. Jack spoke non-stop for the five-minute break, but as soon as the whistle went again they hit us like they did at the start of the match. That Lomu scored his hat-trick after literally a few seconds, with a move that featured Mehrtens chipping over the blind-side, and a quick passing movement. Kronfeld passed to Lomu who did the rest. And when Bachop had scored after 50 minutes it was 35–3, and we were still being overwhelmed. The pressure had been relentless.

At least England then showed some resolve and we started a fight-back to restore some pride. But, the game was over, and the All Blacks knew it. Rory Underwood scored yet another try for England in the fifty-ninth minute, and then skipper Will Carling scored the first of his two solo efforts when his smart chip fell kindly and he went over in the right-hand corner. It was the break we needed, but too little too late. Some critics said that we should have started to run the ball earlier than we did. But we had been so startled by the ferocity and power of the All Black attack that it wasn't easy. At least we showed some mettle.

Jonah Lomu scored his fourth try when he beat Tony Underwood and side-stepped me on the inside. I never laid a finger on him. There were so many All Blacks bearing down on me, that if he hadn't scored one of the others would have done. The conversion made it 42–15, before Will and Rory scored tries for England in the last ten minutes – Rory's second thanks to some great work by Dewi Morris – which restored some respectability to the scoreline.

It had been a brilliant opening spell from a terrific side. I had expected England to test the New Zealanders, and beat them, as they had not been stretched on the run-in to the semi-final. But on the day we could not do it, and having played in that battle, I can say, with some certainty, it will be tough for South Africa in the final next weekend! The New Zealanders are a class act, but they are definitely beatable. You have got to starve them of the ball; you can't give them possession, otherwise you're going to have to do a lot of defending. Springboks take note.

Against England, the All Blacks got their game plan just right – in fact, they got it perfect. They hit us hard early on, took our breath away, and did not kick to touch which might have given us a chance from the line-outs, one of our key strengths. And without the ball, we could not put them under pressure. Admittedly, when we did have the chance our line-out was not up to its usual standard but, having lost our pattern, shape and confidence early on, that was not a surprise. There always appeared to be two or three New Zealand players for every one of us.

It was very good to see that an England side which was 18 points down so near the start of the game could come back with such spirit and win the second half, but it was all over by then. We did come back pretty well when we started to run with the ball; perhaps this clash might in future be regarded as the match which officially signified the end of the northern hemisphere's reliance on the kick-and-chase game. We'll have to wait and see.

One thing is for sure, Lomu is a 'human rhino', as Cooch so eloquently pointed out.

The dressing-room was choked after the game. Will was very disappointed. 'He's a freak,' he said, and 'the sooner he goes away the better!'. Will added that he has never come up against a side that has started like that, and maintained it.

Somehow we'll have to pick ourselves up for the game against France to decide who comes third and fourth on Thursday, but I don't know how. It may appear as a sideshow now, but it is important as the winner will not have to pre-qualify for the next World Cup. But after today's disappointment, it will not be easy. After the huge investment we have made in time and effort, and the dedication we have shown over the last six months – and in some cases longer – it's a real kick in the teeth, especially after winning against Australia in the wonderful way we did last week.

Factfile: England 29 New Zealand 45

- England scorers: R. Underwood, two tries

  W. Carling, two tries

  R. Andrew, three conversions, one penalty.
- The 45–29 defeat was the highest score recorded by a team in a Test against England.
- Zinzan Brooke became the first forward to drop a goal in the history of All Black Test rugby.
- It was the first game I had lost wearing an England shirt.

What the press said

New Zealand were amazing. They have all the strength you expect of an All Black side, but when you have something like that on the left wing, it adds something.

WILL CARLING, TALKING TO THE DAILY EXPRESS, 19 JUNE 1995

When you have someone like that you are in a different league. Without being funny, if you take him out of the game it would have made a huge, huge difference.

WILL CARLING, TALKING TO THE DAILY TELEGRAPH, 19 JUNE 1995

He is a phenomenon . . . someone should have bought him up before the World Cup.

JACK ROWELL, AFTER THE GAME, ON JONAH LOMU, 18 JUNE 1995

I am sure our Prime Minister will put up the Crown Jewels if that is what it takes to keep him in New Zealand.

ALL BLACKS' COACH LAURIE MAINS ON LOMU, QUOTED IN THE DAILY
MIRROR, 19 JUNE 1995

The incredible hulk tore Will Carling's World Cup dream away as though he was tucking into one of his favourite, over-ripe Kiwi fruits.

LOMU – Lethal Object; Massacred Us

COLIN PRICE, THE DAILY MIRROR, 19 JUNE 1995

England's World Cup bid was blown out of the water here at Newlands by Jonah the Whale.

. . . Lomu then powered in on Catt and the England full-back almost went down in subjugation at the big man's feet. Lomu was through him in a trice – and the shattering avalanche followed.

. . . Then Eureka! Rory Underwood replied with England's first try after a jinking run by Catt.

STEPHEN HOWARD, THE SUN, 19 JUNE 1995

It was a hair-raising marvel of a performance from this 6 ft 5in giant of a man, blessed with a strength and physical presence way beyond his 20 years.

    . . . it was also inspiring, a sporting occasion to treasure.

JOHN MASON, THE DAILY TELEGRAPH, 19 JUNE 1995

It took New Zealand less than two minutes to feed Jonah Lomu. The result was a spectacular try and a statement of intent that has prevailed throughout this tournament.

    Lomu excepted, England probably shaded New Zealand in terms of pace and power . . . The missing words were ambition and vision.

STUART BARNES IN THE DAILY TELEGRAPH, 19 JUNE 1995

I would not want to tackle him [Lomu].

SEAN FITZPATRICK, NEW ZEALAND CAPTAIN, AFTER THE GAME,
18 JUNE 1995

The lesson . . . is that unless rugby union can find some commercial accommodation for such players as Lomu, the game will increasingly be no more than a nursery for the serious money elsewhere.

DAVID MILLER, THE TIMES, 19 JUNE 1995

FIFTEEN

Playing for 1999

We went to the Sports Café in Sandton after the game last night and had a few drinks. We were shattered. It's been a long five weeks and I'm mentally exhausted. It's even worse for some of the older players who are either going to retire soon, or will be too old to play again in 1999. They have realised that their last chance of winning the golden Webb Ellis Trophy has gone.

MONDAY, 19 JUNE

We have moved to the Holiday Inn in Pretoria for a few days, as the third and fourth play-off game will take place here on Thursday evening at 5 p.m. I'm looking forward to the French game, Dewi's last match, and hopefully we can beat them convincingly. They were unlucky not to go through to the final in the water-logged semi, and we will be hard pushed to beat them for a ninth successive time. They can really swing the ball about if they are in the mood, but I believe our defeat on Sunday has stung us into action for one last effort.

TUESDAY, 20 JUNE

As the Backgammon championship moved towards its climax (I'm down £49 to John Mallett, and up £1.20 in my contest with Phil de Glanville), the team for Thursday's game against France was announced. Winger Tony Underwood has been dropped in favour of Ian Hunter, probably because he still appears shell-shocked after his confrontation with big Jonah, and number eight Deano is ruled out because of a shoulder injury. Steve Ojomoh takes Dean's place.

It's a shame for Deano, as it means that he will never have had the chance to play against France in the World Cup. He was dropped for the quarter-final against the French in 1991 and he still says it was one of the low points of his rugby career.

Training went well today; the boys seem to have picked themselves up after the defeat against the All Blacks.

WEDNESDAY, 21 JUNE

We are keen to beat the French, and the stakes are high, despite it being a play-off. We don't want to have to pre-qualify for the 1999 World Cup finals hosted by Wales, so the game will not turn out to be a gentle runaround. We're not going to throw away all the hard work and effort we have put into this World Cup campaign just to lose tomorrow. We are a proud team, and want to turn on the style if we can. It is also Dewi's last game before retirement, and he's trying to organise a few more days fun for us at Sun City after the tournament.

Everyone had an individual session with Spook Austin Swain, and some of the players even had an acupuncture session with our team masseur to relax them.

THURSDAY, JUNE 22

• England v France
The play-off for the third and fourth place, at Loftus Versfeld, Pretoria, 5 p.m. kick-off.

ENGLAND
15   M.J. Catt (Bath)
14   I. Hunter (Northampton)
13   W.D.C. Carling (Harlequins)*
12   P.J.C. Guscott (Bath)

* captain

11   R. Underwood (Leicester)
10   C.R. Andrew (Wasps)
9   C.D. Morris (Orrell)
1   J. Leonard (Harlequins)
2   B.C. Moore (Harlequins)
3   V.E. Ubogu (Bath)
4   M.O. Johnson (Leicester)
5   M.C. Bayfield (Northampton)
6   T.A.K. Rodber (Northampton)
7   B.B. Clarke (Bath)
8   S. Ojomoh (Bath)

FRANCE
15   J.-L. Sadourny (Colomiers)
14   E. N'Tamack (Toulouse)
13   P. Sella (Agen)
12   T. Lacroix (Dax)
11   P. Saint-André (Montferrand)*
10   F. Mesnel (Racing)
9   F. Galthie (Colomiers)
1   C. Califano (Toulouse)
2   J.-M. Gonzalez (Bayonne)
3   L. Benezech (Racing)
4   O. Merle (Montferrand)
5   O. Roumat (Dax)
6   A. Benazzi (Agen)
7   L. Cabannes (Racing)
8   A. Cigana (Toulouse)

Referee: D. Bishop

We were so disappointed to finish the tournament on a losing note, defeated by the French 9–19, and well beaten — two tries to nil. After a long five-week tour, and going out to the All Blacks on Sunday, we did not have the energy, will power or initiative to carry us through this final game. We just could not deliver. The dressing-room was silent. When Brian Moore was approached to be 'randomly' drug-tested immediately after the game, I thought he was going to bite the guy's head off. Not only was the defeat hard to swallow, but Brian has seemingly been singled out for these tests since day one. They pushed him just one step too far this time.

We all played badly, well below par, and the packed Pretoria crowd of 44,000, full of England supporters, must have been hugely disappointed with our tepid display. There was no invention. The passing was poor, and the approaches clumsy. We know it, the crowd knows it. Only Dewi Morris, who retires from top-flight rugby today, played a decent game. The England team never got out of the starting blocks, and the first half ended with a dour 3–3 scoreline, one penalty each. There was no fluent running rugby and little heart. Then, after the interval, the French scored two tries in the second half. The first try followed a line-out won by Olivier Merle. The French pack drove on, and the ball carrier by then, Olivier Roumat, went over for the score. The second, scored by N'Tamack late in the game, sealed our fate. He ran smartly through a succession of vain tackles from Dewi, Rory, and myself, and finished off what for us was an awful performance.

I should think the most exciting part of the game for the fans was the prolonged Mexican wave. There wasn't much of a strategy, although we had decided to try and run the ball, and it didn't work. It's very hard to run the ball at international level, particularly against a team like France, which has such a good defence. We didn't get much penetrating movement from the forwards and, as the crowd found out, you can't really play a running game on the back foot. We always seemed to be running backwards. Perhaps England should have stuck to the game we're really comfortable with and good at, the kicking game, especially with Rob Andrew in the side.

We were all down after the match had finished, fully aware that now we've got to pre-qualify for the next World Cup, which will be a challenge in itself. During the tournament, I read one banner which said: 'Watch out for the USA in 1999'. Even they are putting together a rugby team, and who knows . . . Why shouldn't the USA be a force to be reckoned with in years to come? Your guess is as good as mine.

Factfile: England 9 France 19

- England scorers: Andrew, three penalties
- Thierry Lacroix scored nine points, from three penalties, taking his tally for the tournament to 112 and assuming top place in the 1995 World Cup scoring league, eight points ahead of Scotland captain Gavin Hastings.

What the press said

England looked jaded and dispirited from an early point. Maybe this was because, having played at sea level for five matches, they were playing for the first time at 6,000 feet. More likely, I think, it was the scars of that 45–29 mauling by New Zealand in the semi-final that hurt most.

JOHN MASON, THE DAILY TELEGRAPH, 23 JUNE 1995

The Rowell revolution towards more expansive open rugby in the 1995 World Cup died a death in the third place match.

Why could not England just this once and with nothing to lose, have changed their game plan and adopted the attitude, 'if they run two tries, we'll run three'?

Will Carling was right when he said, after yesterday's defeat, that it was a sad occasion. Indeed it was. A team with so much more potential had under-performed; a team so strong, so tactically and defensively watertight, so consistent that many within the South Africa and Australia squads, never mind the English themselves, had expected them to turn over New Zealand. That result was of earthquake proportions for the Five Nations' champions: not just now, but for a long time to come.

DAVID MILLER, THE TIMES, 23 JUNE 1995

FRIDAY, 23 JUNE

It's over and we can let our hair down. Last night was, therefore, the first opportunity of the long tour to stage a serious court session, but as we had lost to France it was, not surprisingly, a bit dour and dry. Judge Damian Hopley still managed to be on top form, and the management was singled out for special punishments. One member of the team had to rub baby cream into himself and pose for the court, while Jack and Les were ordered to don workmen's hats and dungarees for the rest of the day.

Today we set off for one final day in Sun City, with the promise of a late-night party in the staff bar, Zorba's. It's time to relax. Sun City really is like a different world; it's a great place. We stayed at the Baku Bung game lodge for the night, about 15 minutes away from the main complex, but we didn't sleep much in the end. I think we eventually stopped partying at 6 a.m. and there were a few thick heads!

SATURDAY, 25 JUNE AND SUNDAY, 26 JUNE

Just time enough for most of the boys to sober up a bit before the cup final between the Springboks and our tormentors, New Zealand.

I watched the World Cup final at Debbie's house in Johannesburg. I could have got a ticket and gone to the final, and seven or eight of the England team did go to the match, but I chose not to go with them. Perhaps it was just as well, because when the England team arrived at Ellis Park their seats had already been taken! It looked as though the seats had been sold a few times over. With some (gentle) persuasion the England players got their seats back, but I know that some of the French players ended up standing.

The closing ceremony itself was scintillating. The whole atmosphere was great, with President Mandela wearing a Springbok shirt, the SAA plane flying low over the stadium, and the music. The Rainbow nation was as one that afternoon, and the whole country was on the edge of its seat watching the Springboks pinch the crown from the New Zealand All Blacks, 15–12, after the first extra time of the whole tournament. It was an epic game, and worthy of the final. With just eight minutes of extra time to go, fly-half Joel Stransky wrote his name in Springbok folklore with one priceless, winning drop-goal. Had the scores finished level, the All Blacks would have won, by virtue of the fact that the South Africans had a poorer disciplinary record during the cup.

I naturally felt very disappointed watching the final, knowing that it could have been me playing there, for England. But that's rugby, and as we weren't at Ellis Park playing in the game I wanted the Springboks to win, and they undoubtedly deserved to win for playing out of their skins. The South Africans were the better team on the day, with Stransky and the forwards outstanding (the tackling was superb – and so, too, was their strategy for taking Lomu out of the game) and they have played well throughout. Their home support has also been something else.

Despite the well-earned victory, there may be a row brewing already – about food poisoning. Around 27 of the All Blacks went down with what they claim was food poisoning on the Thursday afternoon before the game, and the team has hinted that perhaps someone may have done it on purpose. The New Zealanders are not blaming the upset tums for their performance on Saturday, but they have still decided to 'bring it up' (oops, sorry) in the press. Anything is possible, I suppose, and some of the New Zealanders were playing below par in the cup final. But it's all idle talk now, and nothing can take away from the mighty Springbok performance.

Had All Black Andrew Mehrtens played to the best of his ability and kicked all of his chances, it could have been a different story anyway. It must have been the pressure that told. Until the final, Mehrtens had not been put under any great pressure at all, but he was up against it at Ellis Park, and he's only young. When it comes down to the wire, you need experience, particularly when you're playing against the South African nation as well as their rugby team! In addition, all of those priceless South African characteristics — like competitiveness, aggressiveness and the will to win — came to the fore on the day, and the victory was merited. As for New Zealand dynamo, Andrew Mehrtens, he is a class player, and I am sure he will bounce back even better having played a part in this final.

The closing World Cup Dinner, held at the mammoth Gallagher Estate on the Saturday evening after the game, was a bit like the opening ceremony down in Cape Town, a load of rubbish. It was unnecessary, but it was still compulsory for the four semi-final teams to be there. We were told we had to be there at 7.30 p.m. for 8 p.m., and we were there on time — the first team to arrive. The Springboks didn't arrive until about 9.15 p.m.

There was nothing wrong with the function itself, but we were tired and disappointed, particularly having had to watch the final without playing in it. And the speech by South African rugby chief, Dr Louis Luyt, was something else — completely uncalled for. He intimated that the Springboks would have also been world champions in 1987 and 1991, had they played in the tournaments, and also singled out one referee, Derek Bevan, as the best in the World Cup, and presented him with a special gift. The New Zealanders, in particular, and all of the other match referees, including Ed Morrison, the Englishman who refereed the final, were seemingly very upset, and understandably so. The speech was so embarrassing that some of the Springboks were also appalled. However, Louis Luyt is nothing if not a controversial figure, and it's usually the best policy to laugh off much of what he says.

Sunday, and it's time to break up and go our separate ways after a long and tiring five weeks. Everything has to come to an end. Most of the team set off for Heathrow early this morning, but Tim Rodber and his girlfriend are going on for a sunshine holiday in Mauritius. I'm taking the opportunity to go home to Port Elizabeth for a few days break. I need it.

SIXTEEN

Reflections on the World Cup Experience

Looking back on the South African adventure as a whole, it was a great experience, and I thoroughly enjoyed the World Cup, although I was naturally very disappointed that we lost in the semi-final.

There were highs and lows, as there are on any overseas tour. The start of the trip was very flat, and for much of the time during the pool games in Durban it was quite boring; we were not allowed to do very much — either in terms of training or anything else — because we needed to keep something extra in reserve for later on in the tournament. I was personally disappointed that we were diverted away from the supporters and the media on our arrival, which immediately made everything very low key. While a lot of players don't like a high-profile welcome, I think it's fun, and it would have got us straight into the spirit of the World Cup. We didn't really get that cup fever until the pool games were over, as the atmosphere inside King's Park was also very subdued. However, once we got into the quarter and semi-finals things improved markedly and there was much more excitement wherever we went.

The Rugby World Cup was, nevertheless, a dream come true. To play with my England team-mates on such a special stage, and to play against the best in the world, was marvellous.

I felt I played pretty steadily throughout the tournament, although it wasn't the best tour I could have had. I played very well against Western Samoa and Australia, and I really enjoyed those games, particularly the high-pressure knock-out tie against the Wallabies. I also felt good when I ran out to play against

France, but I couldn't pick my team-mates up that evening and it wasn't to be. The French cut us down to size pretty quickly. Too much of England's play in South Africa was stop-start rugby, and I didn't get too many opportunities to show what I could do. But international rugby is like that, and you have to try and excel every time you do get the ball.

As far as the England team was concerned, I think Dewi played very well, and so, too, did Rob, Martin Johnson and Ben Clarke. But nobody was outstanding, because it was an all-round team effort. Even the super-subs like Phil de Glanville, Jon Callard, John Mallett and Damian Hopley all made the most of their opportunities when they were on the field. Looking outside the England camp, there were some real stars in the tournament; Jonah Lomu, of course, Andrew Mehrtens, Josh Kronfeld, Frank Bunce, Chester Williams and Joel Stransky all gave huge performances for their countries.

The most memorable part of my cup experience was the win against Australia (although in terms of fun, the paint-balling was tremendous!). I was also really pleased that the whole England team got along with each other so well for the testing five-week tour − there was no bitching and no niggling. It was a very close squad and that makes a tour like this one all the more pleasurable. Seeing my family and friends, and being back at home in South Africa, made it extra special.

The card school didn't really get off the ground on this trip, and it was much smaller than we thought it was going to be. We had a big session before the Australian game, and one before the New Zealand semi-final, but that was about it. Backgammon was more popular this time around. John Mallett and Phil de Glanville played their own mini-World Cup, but I did get to play them occasionally. In the end I ended up owing John Mallett £53 and Phil £13.50. I was only in the 'Village Two' league, the Backgammon championship's second division, so I didn't get to play them too much because I wasn't considered good enough, although I did beat them both a few times.

The worst part of the tour, and the lowest point, was losing to France, although we deserved to be beaten. The defeat against New Zealand was also awful. We played the All Blacks on, perhaps, the only day of the tournament when they were truly awesome. Admittedly, our defence wasn't very good that afternoon; they took full advantage, and how. It was so disappointing afterwards when we sat back and took in the reality that we were out of the World Cup.

I think Jack Rowell will probably stay around for another four years and try and win the next William Webb Ellis Trophy. I think he needs to forget about what was, and what could have been, and start again. It was his first World Cup and it will harden him for the next one. I'm looking forward to seeing how he will approach the challenge for the next cup, which will be hosted by Wales in 1999. I'm not sure whether he will be looking to bring new players in immediately, or whether he will give it a year or so before he recruits new ones to the team, allowing himself plenty of time to assess who is capable of playing on the world stage. Will Carling, I know, would be keen to be part of that rebuilding process, but it is early days yet. He played well and was very committed throughout the tournament, and he is one of the main driving forces in the England side. Once again the captain proved he can still produce the goods at this level.

We do have the young players in England capable of beating the All Blacks and the Springboks, but they will have to be nursed properly, and that's not as easy as it sounds. In the UK we don't have the training and development facilities or camps, or the places where good young players are worked hard and brought on, like those in Australia, for instance. We need a more professional approach, and that will probably take money.

Money, professionalism, who mentioned those?

I had heard that executives from Rupert Murdoch's News International — the company which now, in reality, controls the sport of rugby league — had been having unofficial talks with the South African Rugby Union during the Rugby World Cup (and they were probably talking before the tournament as well).

The rumour was that Mr Murdoch was seeking to do the same

with rugby union, focussing on a deal with 'the southern hemisphere' teams. We had heard that he wanted to get the All Blacks, Wallabies, Springboks, Fiji, Tonga, Western Samoa and possibly Argentina formed into a special championship. Then, the rumour went, he would go and have a look at the potential in the northern hemisphere.

It was, therefore, no surprise when it was confirmed that a deal had been struck in the days leading up the World Cup final. There are hundreds of millions of Murdoch pounds in play for the exclusive ten-year broadcasting rights to all major matches involving the key southern hemisphere countries, notably the Springboks, Australia and New Zealand. Professionalism is marching on, and the players from these countries will no doubt see the rewards somewhere, somehow. In one fell swoop it puts the northern hemisphere countries at a distinct disadvantage on the world rugby stage, and now the International Board meeting in August will assume even greater importance than ever. I think the northern hemisphere countries must try and get on the bandwagon, somehow, or else there will be two divisions in world rugby – with the southern hemisphere countries playing in the top division on their own. We are already at least a year behind the southern hemisphere teams in everything we do, especially in terms of developing speed and power. That gap can only widen unless the the northern hemisphere acts quickly.

Rugby union was no less vulnerable than the sport of rugby league was before it got signed up for cash by the Murdoch empire. Money talks. Aussie coach Bob Dwyer commented recently: 'People will see the massive amounts of money being made at the World Cup, the monies generated by television, and they will come to the conclusion that it makes sense.' In hindsight, he was right, of course. According to Michael Herd of *The Evening Standard*, the incumbent English RFU secretary Tony Hallett agrees. Speaking even before the Murdoch deal was signed, he said:

It remains to be seen whether the game can withstand the considerable pressure from the world of commerce that is bound to come after the World Cup. I don't think it is any stronger than rugby league was, but only time will tell. Whatever happens over the money aspect I hope the game still runs itself rather than the businessmen in the years to come. That's what has been so special about rugby union — take that spirit away and much of the magic of the sport could disappear. We don't want to sell the soul of rugby.

I cannot disagree with that.

SEVENTEEN

Back at Home

Sitting quietly in my dad's living-room in Port Elizabeth, the World Cup already seems light years away, and the final was only three days ago.

The future looks as challenging and fascinating as ever. I can't wait for that crucial International Board meeting in August, nor for the start of the new Bath campaign.

Personally, I've been 'signed up' to work with a well-known company called Masters International, who will be representing me off the field. They look after a lot of top South African-born sportsmen, like golfers Ernie Els, Nick Price and cricketer Graham Hick, and it will be interesting and exciting to see what opportunities present themselves, and what opportunities are allowed to present themselves. They are nice people, and I feel very comfortable and at home with them. I'll be doing more coaching, that's for sure, and anything else I can do for the game of rugby union, including visiting schools.

I'm going to have a two-week rest in the sun and then I'm planning to start some serious kicking practice with Dave Alred in Bristol. I've got to put in the hours on my kicking, particularly if I want to try and do it for Bath this season.

After a good break, it should not be too difficult to pick myself up for the new season, particularly as there will be more opportunity to focus on Bath commitments this year. As well as the kicking practice I also need a big pre-season drive on the weights, to further increase my upper-body strength, before I go into the pre-season work with Bath. I don't tend to put weight on when I'm not playing, so that's a bonus, and I'm lucky that I've never struggled with my fitness. I should therefore be in good shape for the start of the English domestic season, and I look forward to it with relish, as I always do. I also look forward to playing for Bath with my scrum-half brother, Richard, who thinks he will be available from December.

It's rugby that has kept me in England since 1992 and I would be happy to stay in the UK for the next ten years if my rugby career thrives and develops. But when it's all over, I'll probably go home to the sunshine of the new South Africa to be with my family and friends again. I've never thought for one moment that I would stay in England for ever. I may now be English, but South Africa is still home. Nevertheless, I feel a strong sense of loyalty towards England, because the country and the people have been so good to me, and they have helped me achieve rugby ambitions that I only dreamed about in South Africa. The fans and the players here in England, and in Bath in particular, have been wonderful. But it's the thrill of the game of rugby union I really stayed in England for. It's the game that I love, and would do anything for, anywhere.

Mike Catt's England Record

19 Mar 1994	Wales	Twickenham	Won 15–8
10 Dec 1994	Canada	Twickenham	Won 60–19 2 tries

FIVE NATIONS CHAMPIONSHIP 1995

21 Jan 1995	Ireland	Lansdowne Road	Won 20–8
04 Feb 1995	France	Twickenham	Won 31–10
18 Feb 1995	Wales	Cardiff Arms Park	Won 23–9
18 Mar 1995	Scotland	Twickenham	Won 24–12

WORLD CUP 1995 – SOUTH AFRICA

27 May 1995	Argentina	King's Park, Durban	Won 24–18
31 May 1995	Italy	King's Park, Durban	Won 27–20
04 June 1995	Western Samoa	King's Park, Durban	Won 44–22 1 drop goal
11 June 1995	Australia	Newlands, Cape Town	Won 25–22
16 June 1995	New Zealand	Newlands, Cape Town	Lost 29–45
22 June 1995	France	Loftus Versfeld, Pretoria	Lost 9–19

Mike Catt — Bath 1st XV Appearance Record

Season	Total	Courage League	Pilkington Cup	Friendlies
1992–93	9	1	—	8
1993–94	23	14*	5	4
1994–95	19	14	4	1
Total	51	29	9	13

* 1 as replacement

Mike Catt — Bath 1st XV Scoring Record — All Games

Season	Tries	Conversions	Penalties	Drop Goals	Total points
1992–93	6	8	1	—	49
1993–94	9	6	6	—	75
1994–95	2	4	3	5	42
Total	17	18	10	5	
Total points	85	36	30	15	166